T0244872

# the
# Day
## that turns
## your life
## around

**SOUND WISDOM BOOKS BY JIM ROHN**

*The Power of Ambition*

*The Art of Exceptional Living*

*Take Charge of Your Life*

*Unshakable*

*The Day That Turns Your Life Around*

How One Decision Can
Shape Your Destiny

the

# Day

that turns
your life
around

## JIM ROHN

An Official Nightingale-Conant Publication

© Copyright 2024– Jim Rohn

All rights reserved. This book is protected by the copyright laws of the United States of America. No part of this publication may be reproduced, stored in, or introduced into a retrieval system, or transmitted, in any form or by any means (electronic, mechanical, photocopying, recording, or otherwise), without the prior written permission of the publisher. For permissions requests, contact the publisher, addressed "Attention: Permissions Coordinator," at the address below.

Published and distributed by:
SOUND WISDOM
P.O. Box 310
Shippensburg, PA 17257-0310
717-530-2122

info@soundwisdom.com

www.soundwisdom.com

While efforts have been made to verify the information contained in this publication, neither the author nor the publisher assumes any responsibility for errors, inaccuracies, or omissions. While this publication is chock-full of useful, practical information, it is not intended to be legal or accounting advice. All readers are advised to seek competent lawyers and accountants to follow laws and regulations that may apply to specific situations. The reader of this publication assumes responsibility for the use of the information. The author and publisher assume no responsibility or liability whatsoever on behalf of the reader of this publication.

The scanning, uploading, and distribution of this publication via the Internet or via any other means without the permission of the publisher is illegal and punishable by law. Please purchase only authorized editions and do not participate in or encourage piracy of copyrightable materials.

ISBN 13 TP: 978-1-64095-487-8

ISBN 13 eBook: 978-1-64095-488-5

For Worldwide Distribution, Printed in the U.S.A.

1 2 3 4 5 6 7 8 / 28 27 26 25 24

# CONTENTS

# FOREWORD

There is a day, seemingly like any other, when everything changes. It's the day when you decide once and for all to walk a new road toward the goals that, until that fateful day, have only been misty dreams. It's the day when you say, "I've had it with living a life of poor health, an empty bank account, and broken promises." When you're suddenly filled with the resolve to do whatever it takes to finally live the life you have always known you are capable of living.

It's the day when you're filled with the awareness that time is precious, and with each day that passes by unnoticed, it is like releasing a helium balloon into the sky. Too soon, it will be a distant memory, never to be seen again. It's the day you decide to seize every precious moment and make each one count.

*It's the day that turns your life around.*

At the young age of 25, Jim Rohn, master motivator and business philosopher, met his mentor, Earl Shoaff, who introduced him to a unique business opportunity in the world of network marketing. Not only did Mr. Shoaff mentor Jim on the lessons of building a remarkable business, he mentored him on building a remarkable life.

Jim used the lessons he learned to turn away from a life of mediocre performance, broken dreams, and an empty bank account to incredible levels of wealth, both tangible and intangible, by the age of 31. His classic wisdom in this book will help you do the same. Jim Rohn shares ideas in a way you have never heard before. Jim begins by discussing the simple yet dramatic events of his own life-changing day.

While life-changing days can be as cataclysmic as never touching another drop of alcohol or as simple as lying to a Girl Scout, every life-changing day holds something in common—all involve an internal battle inside our head, a battle that must be won.

As the author says, to win the battle in your own mind, you must trust the law of averages, that circumstances will work in your favor, and that your life-changing efforts will be rewarded. Well, there's an old saying that if you can't find the circumstances you want, it's up to you to make them.

Jim expands on this idea by showing you how to move beyond mere faith to begin the process of changing any area of your life for the better.

The key is to begin.

Nightingale-Conant Corporation

# 1

# PUTTING LIFE IN ORDER

One day, I met a young, successful, wealthy businesswoman in New York. She was the vice president of the company, although she never finished her high school education. Interested in her story, I asked her, "How did you get here? This is a tough business. You make big money. You didn't graduate from high school. What happened?"

She said, "Well, let me tell you part of the story. Years ago, one day, I asked my husband for ten dollars, and he said, 'What for?' By the end of that day, I had promised myself that I would never ever ask for money again."

She said, "Yes, I am the vice president. Yes, I do make big money. Yes, I am young. Yes, I did not graduate from high school. But I promise you, Mr. Rohn, from that day until this, I have never asked for money again."

She said, "I started searching for an opportunity, found it, started taking some classes, learned the skills, totally changed my life."

I'm sure she would say that was one of the days that turned her life around.

I firmly believe the saying, "There's nothing so powerful as an idea whose time has come." And also, "There's nothing so powerful as an idea that comes at the right time."

I say a little prayer before speaking to audiences, "I hope today is one of those right times for many in my audience." And I pray the same for you, dear reader. I never know when, for someone, it's the first time or if I'm the first voice that awakens a search for a better life, meaning skills or disciplines. I may be one of many voices you may have heard before; when reading this book right now, the lights may go on and you will never be the same again.

Sometimes, a delightful experience or a tragic experience can be the day that changes everything. For me, it was the Girl Scout who knocked on my door when I was 25 years old and gave me a big presentation about Girl Scout cookies that she wanted me to buy. She said with a big smile, "It's only two dollars, several flavors." I wanted to but, big problem, I didn't have $2 in my pocket, so I didn't want to tell her that, right?

At the time, I was 25 years old, a grown man. I had been to one year of college. I even had a little family going. Yet I decided the next best thing to do was to lie to her.

I said, "Look, I already have lots of Girl Scout cookies. I've bought some and we still haven't eaten all of them. They're in the house."

She said, "Oh, that's wonderful. Thank you very much." She leaves.

Then I said to myself, "I don't want to live like this anymore. I mean, how low can I get right? Lying to a Girl Scout? That's about as low as it gets." I promised myself that day it would never happen again. That was a life-changing day for me.

Recognizing that I was not in a good position, I started my search to get my life in order.

Or take, for instance, another example. A guy climbs the stairs, there are about 40 of them, and he finally gets to the top. He sits down and he's out of breath, so he says, "Wow, this isn't good. I have to do something about my health. I'm not going to be out of breath anymore." It can be something that simple. He starts a little research program and decides to get his health in order, develop a good nutritional program, exercise, whatever. The day that turned his life around!

Sitting at the yacht club having a drink, sort of in a fog one day, my friend David woke up and said, "What could I really have done if I hadn't been in this condition the last fifteen to twenty years of my life?" He wasn't an out-and-out alcoholic, but he drank too much, and he started thinking about what he could have really accomplished if he hadn't been in a stupor most of every day.

He wasn't bad enough to where he couldn't function, but he said that day when he thought back on what he really could have done if he hadn't stumbled around in a bit of a fog all those years how his life would be.

From that day on, he never touched another drink of alcohol. He died about five years after that, but his wife said to me, "The last five years were the greatest years of our marriage. When that one day, he woke up and said, "Wow, this isn't good. What could I have done if I hadn't been sort of semi-conscious these last twenty years?"

That was a very special day for him. Sometimes it's a cataclysmic event. Sometimes it's just a moment. Who can really explain it? Only the person it happens to, I guess, can really explain the inner voice that tells us, "I'm on the wrong track here. I wonder what I could really do if I kicked this habit or got rid of this obsession." Those are the days that turn your life around.

## RIGHT VERSUS WRONG

We live in a world where opposites are in conflict, and we're in the middle. There's the pull to do good and the pull to do evil, to do what's right and the pull to cross the line. That bit of warfare goes on daily in our head, our consciousness. When I was a little kid growing up, I remember a cartoon of a little boy with a little devil on one shoulder and a little angel on the other shoulder. The little devil said to the little boy, "Go ahead and do it. It'll be okay. It'll be fine. Go ahead, go ahead." Little angel was saying, "No, no, no, don't do it. Don't do it." Little devil said, "Yes, go ahead." Little angel voice, "No, no."

I guess that's part of everyone's life experience. It's part of the adventure. The old prophet said, "Love good and hate evil." If we become educated in that way, knowing when the voice of temptation is not the right road to take, we make some better choices.

When I woke up this morning, a little voice said, "You really don't have to do your exercises today. You could skip today. You have some work to do." I got in at about one o'clock this morning on my flight from Colorado Springs. And first thing, that little voice said, "You don't have to do them this morning, you're tired." But I know that if I postpone a day, sure enough, it will be the beginning of a slippery slope, which leads to no exercises. To make up for the late arrival and lack of sleep, I chose to do a modified version of my exercise routine. If I don't have quite enough time, I do something. Don't give in to the little devil.

We all have fairly constant right-versus-wrong decisions to make. We have to choose what voice to listen to. I guess part of the answer is not to become a victim of yourself. Beware of the thief on the street who is after your purse, but also beware of the thief in your mind that's after your promise.

The little thief in your head that says, "You're too tall, you're too short, you've never done it before, it's not going to happen for you. Others can find this book, you can't find it. If you found it, you probably wouldn't read it. If you read it, you probably wouldn't understand it." This is a common bit of warfare going on inside our heads, and we all have to deal with it.

## THE GREAT ADVENTURE

I call these experiences "the great adventure." It seems as though God has designed human life and His own existence as a bit of adventure. For example, He created all the angels, according to the storyteller. And we might surmise that maybe He didn't want to be alone or maybe He wanted to create some adventure for Himself—because He made one of the angels, the most famous and the most beautiful, the leader. Then this angel, Lucifer, gathers up a third of the angels, makes a move on God's throne and loses, giving us a bit of insight but not much detail. I guess most of it is left to our imagination, which is probably what the storyteller wanted to create.

It seems that in the beginning, even before the beginning, God was interested in adventure, but I guess if you boil it down to something very simple, it makes us wonder, "Would it be possible to win if you couldn't lose?" Almost everybody says, "Well, no. It doesn't seem possible that you could win if you couldn't lose." There has to be an adventure to have a victory, to have a win, overcome, and to create something of value. You must keep pulling positively against the negative forces—which creates the adventure!

If you took a football today and walked out to the football stadium, put it under your arm and crossed the goal line, would we all cheer and call it a touchdown? The answer is no. It's not a touchdown until you face the 300-pounders who want to smash your face into the turf—if you can muscle by them, dance by the secondary, and then cross the goal line with the football under your arm. Now, we call it a touchdown, maybe a championship, but not without the conflict, which is a good phrase. Opposites are in conflict, and we're in the middle. On any given day or occasion, that conflict can occur.

There's an interesting Bible story that says there were two nice people, according to the storyteller. The adventure begins when one person builds his house on the rock, and the other builds his house on the sand. Nice people can make foolish decisions about the future and then suffer the consequences, especially when the storms come.

The key is to try your best, not your worst. Many questions are not a matter of morality, it's a question of being careless or careful, being cautious rather than reckless, but not too cautious. It's an interesting challenge to balance between right and wrong during the great adventure.

If you are too cautious driving on a two-way highway, every time a car came your way, you would worry whether or not it was going to stay on its side of the line, so you would pull off the road, wait for it to pass, then get back on the road and continue your journey. That is being too cautious. It may take you two or three days to get to your destination, which is only a few miles away.

When the traffic is coming your way on a two-way highway, you must trust at least the law of averages that says, "I have a pretty good chance of arriving at my destination, even though there's no guarantee that the one out of a thousand coming my way will cross the line and that will be the end of me." We do have to be cautious, but not too cautious. We have to allow our daily experiences to lead us into a better month, a better year, a better life.

## FAITH AND THE LAW OF AVERAGES

The plane I was on was approaching our destination and the flight attendant announced, "Ladies and gentlemen, you have now completed the safest part of your journey. From now on, it gets dangerous. Fasten your seatbelt." I thought that was an interesting announcement. You've now completed the safest part of your journey; according to statistics, for the miles covered, it's the safest way to travel.

Now, you have to be cautious, but not overly cautious, but not obsessively careful. It might be safer just to huddle in your house and stay home, but you can't do that. You have to get out and participate in life and trust that today, the law of averages, hopefully, is going to work in your favor. We all have work to do, so we must get up and get going.

Why would the farmer put the plow in the ground in the spring if he couldn't see the vision of the harvest when fall arrives? Is it possible to see the finished harvest? The answer is yes. We see it simply by faith. Faith is the ability to see things that don't yet exist and that's how things exist. The day that turns your life around is the day you can see by faith the better life right around the corner waiting for you!

# Key phrase:
# Faith is the ability to see things that don't yet exist.

How did that hotel get here? Someone saw it while the lot was vacant. So, is it possible to see a hotel or house or store when all you see today is a vacant lot? The answer is yes, of course.

If somebody can't see the future in their mind's eye, it will never materialize in reality. It's possible to see things that don't yet exist. Interesting, right? So when should you start building your hotel? This is a good question for your philosophical musings. When should you start building your house?

So when should you start? Here's the answer, as soon as it's finished. You wouldn't start building the house until you had finished the project in your mind first. You plan it all out down to the finest detail, and by faith, you will complete it.

If you just start laying bricks with no plan and no faith, and somebody comes by and asks, "What are you doing?"

You would say, "I'm laying bricks."

And then the guy asks, "What are you building?"

You would have to say, "I have no idea."

With faith to see the finished result, it's possible to finish something before you start. In fact, it would be a bit foolish to start until you had it finished. Human beings have the remarkable ability to finish something and then start it. We've heard the old expression, "Don't count your chickens before they're hatched." But no, we actually have the ability to count our chickens long before they're hatched because we have faith. We use the law of averages. There's bound to be at least so many out of every dozen, out of every 100, out of every 50 that will hatch if we have put the right circumstances in place.

## SEEING THE FUTURE

It's possible to see the end before you begin. Start looking into the future of what you would like to accomplish, where you would like to go, the person you would like to be, and envision a clear picture of the finished objective. See yourself there. See yourself in possession of your future.

For a while, I was in business with Bob Cummings, a film and television actor. He said to me, "Decide what you want and then act as if you already have it." Being an actor, he could give good tips on acting. I echo his advice to you, "Decide what you want and act as if it is already yours."

The reason we can act and think that it's already ours is because not only can we envision the end results, we can also envision the beginning of making it real. We don't start until it's finished, but it is possible for human beings to finish something before they start.

Humans are the only life on earth that has the incredible capacity to change the course of our lives. No other life form can do that. All other life forms, except humans, seem to operate simply by instinct in their genetic code.

For example, before winter, the goose flies south. If you said to the goose, "Hey, it'd be better this year to go west," he would ignore that advice. He cannot make choices and cannot listen to advice that contradicts his instinct and genetic code—even if it may be better. He has to obey his inherent instincts.

Not so for human beings, who can alter the course of their lives. Humans can live one way for five years, then tear up that script and live a totally different lifestyle the next five years.

In my case, the first six years of my economic life, I wound up broke. The second six years, I wound up rich. How did I do that? I discovered I wasn't a goose.

You don't have to live the next six years like you did the past six. You can use all the information and all the advice and repair all of your mistakes and adopt a new and refined philosophy—so that the next six years can be totally different from the last six. No other life form can do this.

If you were a tree, you'd be stuck. As a tree, if you used up all the nourishment that was around you and you couldn't change location, you would die. But that's not true for you. You can change location. Go north, south, east, west, live here for a while, live somewhere else for a while. Soak up "nourishment" from a variety of places, people, and careers.

# Key phrase: You can greatly alter the course of your life.

## DESIGNED DESTINATION

Now, here's the next note to make. Five years from now, you will arrive. The question is where. This advice is for mature people now: if you keep up your present disciplines and keep up your present pace, where will you be in five years? Boy, it's easy to say, "Hey, I haven't really thought about that." In five years, here's the probability: you will either arrive at a well-designed destination or an undesigned destination. Well-designed or undesigned, it's your choice.

Five years from now, you really don't want to arrive at an undesigned destination because you may very well wind up wearing what you are wearing today, driving the same vehicle you're driving today, living where you don't want to live, and probably doing what you don't want to do—simply because you didn't design a better destination for yourself.

# Key phrase: Decisions are easy to make—good and bad.

After making bad decisions early in life, it becomes harder to make the right decisions. It's harder to repair our mistakes and get back on track. If you've neglected your health for 10 years, I'm telling you it will take more than 10 days to get it back.

So here's the key: if you start early—right now—making the right decisions, fortune belongs to you. When you start early, all fortunes are available to you—the promise looms large and the odds are heavy in your favor.

# Key phrase:
# Start today making future-wise decisions.

Yes, it's possible to make some radical changes starting late in life and still arrive at your destination with some good treasures. But when people think they don't have much time left, they are not willing to make drastic changes; they believe they're too tired and too weary. Some say, "Look, I don't have much time left. It's not going to happen for me anyway." It's easy to take that attitude. But that is a bad decision. I'm fairly certain that you have at least the next 5 to 10 years ahead of you.

Maybe you have the next 20 years, the next 30 years to repair the errors of the past and set up new disciplines. I'm telling you, making good decisions along your journey to reach a well-designed destination is going to change everything. Five years from now, I wish for you to arrive at a place of productivity, a place that will make you feel good about yourself, a place that will give you honor and respect. A place that will give you influence to touch other people five years from now that you couldn't do today. Where will you be in five years?

# Key phrase: You go in the direction you face.

If you start designing something at the end of this direction, sure enough, you will start going in the direction you face because you will face the direction you design.

## DIRECTION DETERMINES DESTINATION

Direction determines your destination. Destination is not determined by hope. It's not determined by wish. Destination is determined by direction. You can't change your destination overnight, which means you can't arrive in a different place tomorrow. But here's what you *can* change today and over-night—you can change *direction*.

It is so fascinating what a small change of direction will do. Let's say that you're in a comfortable job but with no opportunity for advancement. If you choose not to change direction, in five years from now, you'll wind up in that same comfortable job with no chance of advancement, watching life pass you by.

But...you can arrive at a new destination when you change direction. Maybe that means learning a new skill, changing an unhealthy behavior, bringing order into your life. When you make the right decisions, you can get back on the track, which leads to a much more satisfying, exciting, and productive life.

Your life will take a positive and dramatic turn with just a few wise decisions in discipline, learning, a change of behavior or habits and setting goals—areas that you may have let drift away. That's what I realized at age 25, so I immediately changed my direction, and very quickly I headed in the right direction. And in less than seven years, I was a millionaire. When I met my mentor, I determined my destination.

## A BETTER PLACE

Where would I have been in five or six years if I didn't change direction? Okay, my kids probably wouldn't have been starving and maybe we would've had a place to live—but the joy of productivity and the excitement of becoming valuable to the marketplace and more available to my family and my friends—all of that probably would've escaped me if I would not have changed direction.

I'm so thankful for the circumstances that occurred as a result of making the necessary repairs in my life and choosing to make wise decisions. Sometimes, I can't even imagine the chain of events, circumstances, and situations that happen to bring us to where we are in our day-to-day living.

This had to happen and this had to happen, and this door had to close and this door had to open, and all of those things for me to achieve what I achieved—and even for you to be reading this book. That's part of life's mystery, and we let it be a mystery. We don't even try to figure it out. We just say, "Wow, it's incredible."

So how should we collectively and individually affect each other's lives? By studying, learning, teaching, shaking hands, trading stories, and other things to help people as well as ourselves to make the necessary changes in the journey to our well-designed destination via a new and better direction.

Guess how quickly you can change your health by eating an apple a day? Mama said, "An apple a day keeps the doctor away." Let's say you've been ill long enough, and you've had health problems long enough, and you say, "That's it. That's over. I'm going to start a program now." You don't have to completely revolutionize your entire health life; just start with an apple a day.

You say, "Is it that simple to change my health from bad to good?" The answer is yes. The key is to *start*.

It's not like reading a book about good health and you get halfway through and it says, "Dear reader, set this book aside.

Fall down on the floor and see how many pushups you can do."

Then it goes on to say, "Now, if you haven't done any push-ups, why not just give this book away? You're not going to make the effort to get healthy anyway!" Come on, that's not what I'm encouraging you to do. You don't have to radically change your habits on day one. You can gain momentum and make changes as you go. *Just start.*

Here's what happens when you start going in a new direction: self-esteem will accelerate, and how you feel about yourself will pick up speed all along the way. It doesn't take much for you to feel good about yourself. Actually, just committing to a new direction will make you feel better. And even committing to eating an apple a day is the start to having a health program to make you healthier for the next 20 years.

All you have to do is munch on that first apple. You don't have to announce it to the world, but as you munch on that delicious apple, say, "This is the beginning of developing a health program that will make me healthy. I'll have the vitality to do whatever I want to do for the next 30 years of my life." Munch, munch, happy, happy self-esteem off the scale.

Now, when you eat an apple the second day, you become almost delirious, saying, "Wow, I'm on my way!"

Delirious after eating just two apples? Yes! Not only did you do it yesterday, you've done it again today! You're proving to yourself with no audience, no microphones, no nothing, just you and yourself. You've convinced yourself, "I'm on my way to becoming the healthiest I ever have been. I'm starting a new life. This is the second day. I'm on my way!" That's how easy it is to positively change your life. You don't need some dramatic vision, just begin something. Maybe by health or learning or whatever you need to do to get on track to a better future.

# Key phrase:
# Take a small step to a big change in direction.

I'll tell the story of Lydia Colon, who started her business with a dollar. When she made her first sale, she didn't have any product to deliver. She had to take the customer's money, go get the product, then return and deliver it. But she said, "When I figured out how to do that successfully, my ambition soared. Not at the end of the year of some major huge accomplishment, but just at the end of one struggle with ingenuity to try to figure it out. I showed the person the brochure, and she wanted the product. Then I told her my story about why I didn't have any, but that I would deliver the product, and in turn, I would make a small profit."

That was the day that turned her life around. After figuring out the procedure, which is probably not more than 30 to 40 minutes long, her ambition soared, and she realized, "If I did this once, I can do it again, and then I can do it again!"

It doesn't take some huge year-long project of achievement for your ambition to soar or your confidence to catch fire. All it takes is some attention to detail. Figure out something. Use your ingenuity. Let your skill level reach up to meet what ambition you have at the moment, and sure enough, it all changes. Your life can take on a whole new dimension.

The day you say, "I'm going to make a change to my diet to improve my health," is the day your attitude will change. The day you start with eating your first apple, your self-esteem will change. And you can honestly say, "I'm on my way. I'm never going to be the same again. I'm not going to walk the same old road anymore. I'm going a new way." It doesn't take much to change direction. An apple a day can do it! Do something simple—commit to it, do it, and say, "I'm making the changes that need to be made to turn my life around."

One day, I posed an interesting question to a group, "Could a young boy, eight or nine years old, buy a bottle of soap for two dollars and sell it for three?" They all agreed that "Yes, he could go next door, say, 'Mrs. Brown, I have this soap that Mom uses. It's the best. She says you'll get great results. It's only $3.'"

Mrs. Brown says, "Well, Johnny, I have plenty of soap."

He says, "You better let me come in and check." You don't have to teach kids sales, right? I mean, they're automatic salesmen.

The group all agreed that a child could buy a bottle of soap for two dollars and then sell it for three. Now let me pose some other interesting questions: Will the boy do it? Well, that remains to be seen; even if he could, will he? That's true for all of us. We all could, but will we?

Then I ask, should he do it? That's a good debate topic. They all agreed that we eliminate whether or not he could and started talking about whether or not he should, or whether or not he will, which always remains to be seen. Interesting, right? It's not a matter of whether or not we can—it's if we will or should.

An average person of average intelligence living in this incredible country can become financially independent in a fairly reasonable amount of time. The question is not whether or not they can; the question is whether or not they will. Then the big question is whether or not they should.

Well, you should if you could, but that's not the answer in everybody's life. Is it?

The process of life change is not a matter of ability; it is merely a matter of will. Everyone *can,* but not everyone *will* make the decision to be the one who will stand apart in life— to be transformed into the life they envision. A life beyond the same, the mediocre.

Are you ready to choose the area of your life where you know you need to walk a new road? Be it improving your financial standing, health, family relationships, career moves, whatever. If you have that area in mind, the next chapter gives you steps to transformation and brings together everything that's been discussed thus far.

Now, you will learn how to turn nothing into something.

# 2

# HOW TO TURN NOTHING INTO SOMETHING

I t is said that a sower went out to sow his seed, and sure enough, during the day, seed fell onto the ground. Some of the seeds fell on good soil and some on not-too-good soil. Therefore, some seeds produced 30 percent, some 60 percent, and some 100 percent. We say, well, that's just the way things are.

Someone may ask, "With the help of some soil enrichment, couldn't the ones doing 30 percent do 60 or 100 percent?" Well, maybe so, but will the sower provide the enrichment? It remains to be seen.

## FROM SEEDS TO SALES

You may say, "Sales have never appealed to me. I couldn't buy a bottle of soap for two dollars and sell it for three." But what if you had to support your family? "Well, I probably could figure out how to do it if I had to." It's amazing how easy the answer is to solving problems, earning money, making money, and doing better. Everybody can, but not everybody will. I call it the magic and the mystery. The magic is you can start at the bottom and go to the top. The mystery is why wouldn't everybody do that?

Living in our opportunities-abundant country, there are so many examples everywhere of what properly channeled ambition can do that it hardly leaves anyone with an excuse not to at least try. It can be done. It certainly is possible to start with a dollar and become a millionaire. It is certainly possible to start with nothing and become something.

I've been studying a subject recently: how to turn nothing into something. Here's a little gist of what I've been covering.

*First,* to turn nothing into something, you start with ideas and imagination. Now, it's hard to call ideas and imagination nothing. How tangible are ideas and imagination? It's a bit of a mystery. Ideas can be turned into a hotel, ideas can be turned into an enterprise, ideas can be turned into a vaccine, and ideas can be turned into miracle products. What you imagine can turn into ideas.

An idea in itself isn't tangible. It isn't like a house or a desk. But to turn the intangible into something, you start with imaginative ideas. Interesting, right? Ideas that become so powerful in your mind and your consciousness that they seem real to you even before they become tangible. Imaginations that are so strong you can actually see the results.

When I built my first home for my family in Idaho many years ago, before I started construction, I took my friends and associates to the vacant property and gave them a tour through the house. Is that possible? Is it possible to take someone on a tour through an imaginary house? The answer is yes. I would say, "This is where my three-car garage will be."

And the guy would look around and say, "Yes, this garage will hold three cars." I could make my idea real, make it live.

Then "inside" the house, I would point and say, "Here's the double-sided fireplace. It is brick on one side and stone on the other side." I could make it real. As we walked through the rest of the house, I'd say, "Here's the kitchen with this view window over the sink," and they would look out the window as I took them on this tour. One day, I made this house so real, one of my friends bumped his elbow on the fireplace. I mean, it was so real.

Imaginative ideas can't be held because they aren't tangible, but they can come alive in our minds and become almost real. *The first step is to imagine the possibilities.* Make every situation a learning experience—absorb what you hear and see at seminars and classes, during sermons and testimonials, when singing song lyrics—life gives us ideas of the possibilities every day. Imagine the possibilities.

# Key phrases: **Imagine the possibilities.** Imagine the possibilities are possible for you!

*Second,* to turn nothing into something, believe that what you imagine is possible for you to achieve. We become supported by testimonials that say something like, "If I can do it, you can do it." Believe it! First, we imagine what's possible. Second, we start to believe that what's possible is possible for us.

We might also believe it because of our own testimonials. Our personal testimonials might be, "Because I did it once, I can do it again." And "If it happened to me before, it could very well happen again." Or "Because we did it last year, we can do it this year." Those statements are very powerful. They're not actual substance, although they're very close. One is to imagine the possibilities. Two is to imagine that what's possible is possible for you. That second step is the *faith to believe.*

It's said that "Faith is substance." An interesting word that is the powerful ability to believe in the possibilities that are possible for you if you have faith to believe that faith is substance. Substance meaning a piece of the real. Now, it's not real; it's not the podium, but it is so powerful that it's so close to being real. The writer said, "The faith is a piece of, the substance of," and then he called it evidence, substance and evidence. It's difficult to call substance and evidence nothing. It is nothing in the sense that it can't be seen except with the inner eye.

You can't get a hold of it because it isn't yet tangible, but it is possible to turn to nothing, especially ideas and imagination. Now, if you believe that it's possible for you, that substance and evidence become so powerful that it can now be turned into reality. The first step is to imagine what's possible. Second step is to believe that what's possible is possible for you.

*Third,* to turn nothing into something, the third step is to *go to work and make it real.* You go to work and build a hotel. You go to work and make it an enterprise. You go to work and enjoy good health. You go to work and develop a good marriage. You now go to work and make good decisions. You make your ideas tangible and viable. You breathe life into the possibility, and then you construct it.

That is such a powerful ability for us humans. I wanted to take the time to drop in that piece of truth of how to turn nothing into something before I move on to so many other important subjects.

# Key phrase: Faith invested into activity creates reality.

*Fourth,* it takes disciplined activity to turn nothing into something. Faith without the activity serves no useful purpose, but *faith invested into the activity creates reality.*

Once I understood that, I knew then it was possible to build a career. I knew it was possible to build good health. I knew it was possible to build good relationships. I knew I could participate in constructing valuable associations, valuable enterprises, valuable entities that would help and benefit other people. I knew I could be part of it, and I knew I could do it once I understood this formula.

# Key phrase:
# Appreciate the disciplines that turn imagination into reality.

Here's the last part: *appreciate the disciplines that turn imagination into reality*—because without the disciplines, it doesn't work. Discipline is the last piece of the miracle process. The last piece of the miracle process is to do the work, to do the work of good health, to do the work of a relationship, to do the work of building this hotel.

## NEW LIFE RECIPE

In the first chapter, you learned about the immense power that a single day holds for turning around any area of your life, and you discovered that the journey to an entirely new life destination begins with surprisingly small actions mixed with faith. In this chapter, we get much more specific by outlining the major ingredients of emotions and philosophies that comprise a recipe called a new life.

First, we discuss a negative emotion that, if channeled properly, can lead to incredibly positive results. Disgust is such a negative emotion, but...

Remember my little story about the Girl Scout when I said, "I don't want to live like this anymore." That was a traumatic day for me. I was a grown man with a family. I wasn't destitute, but I was behind on paying my bills, and once in a while I'd get a notice saying, "You told us the check was in the mail." Those were embarrassing moments. But the day I lied to that little girl was the climax—the event that turned my life around. I was disgusted with myself.

Whatever disgusting, never-again circumstance you may face—it may be exactly the one that changes your decision-making process for a lifetime. Some decisions are incremental; you make the valuable decision to start the process. Then later you make the decision to continue making good decisions that make a positive difference. You will think, *That felt good. That got good results. Why not continue?*

At age 25, when I really started revolutionizing, especially my economic life, the early successes locked me in for a lifetime. I realized such great early returns. I don't mean overnight, but at the end of the first week, but at the end of the first month, I started a small part-time venture and reaped big results. Opportunities are available to all of us.

My new life recipe included my decision to read books. I started a program of reading. Now, I have one of the best libraries of anyone I know. This was a life-changing decision that lasted a lifetime. We need a little help, a little association with others and gleaning wisdom from those who are already successful.

## CAMARADERIE

Four of the most powerful words in the world are *let's go do it*. It's powerful to say "I'm going to do it," but it's even more powerful to say, "Let's go do it." Sometimes, partnering with someone of like mind will move you farther and faster toward your goal.

For example, if you want to improve your health, it's good to say, "I'm going to do it!" But it might be even better to say to a spouse, friend, or colleague, "Let's do it together. Let's meet every Tuesday and Thursday morning at the gym and work out for an hour." Or "Let's meet at Denny's for lunch once a week and talk over our exercise regime. We can ask each other how we're doing." I think that's a valuable way to achieve your goal—being accountable to someone brings the best results.

Or how about, "Let's get better educated. I'll read a book over the next two weeks and you read a book too. Then we'll get together and talk about both books. Okay, let's do it!" You may not do it by yourself, but if you have somebody like-minded and committed to improvement, you're most likely to follow through. An ancient phrase says, "If two or three agree on a common purpose, nothing is impossible."

The inspiration of camaraderie is that working together with a few others makes a huge difference. In all of my successful enterprises, multiple people were involved—two, three, four, five, six others. We were all on the same page; "Let's do it," is such a powerful motivator. Resolve says, "Do it or die. I'll continue until I see results." Resolve is willing to face the unknown. But at times, readjustments need to be made.

It's like planting corn seed in an acre of ground that doesn't produce a harvest the first year. You may try again the next year because you are resolved to continue. And in the second year, there is no harvest. Now, you need to consider the problem, read about it, confer with experts, and then resolve to make an adjustment. Perhaps the soil was not conducive to corn and another crop will be successful. Perhaps the corn seed was the issue. Learning to make adjustments in your pursuit is wise.

## PHILOSOPHICAL ADJUSTMENTS

I had to make several philosophical changes when I chose to walk a new road at age 25. No doubt you will too—no matter your age. These same philosophies can also make a big difference in your life.

# Key phrase: Profits are better than wages.

The following are some of the philosophies that changed my life forever. Here's the first one: *profits are better than wages.* Once I understood that, I got rich. Nobody taught me that in high school. I went to college for a year and a half, and I never heard it there either.

Wages make you a living, which is fine. But profits make you a fortune, which is super fine. I taught this reality in Moscow when I was teaching about capitalism. The communists had it all wrong. They taught that capitalism was a big company that oppresses its workers—which was and still is an absolutely ridiculous philosophy. Communism taught that capital (financial resources) belongs to the state (government), not the people. We taught that capital belongs in the hands of the people, not the state.

That's why, of course, we pay taxes to help finance the country's infrastructure, for instance. All capitalists should pay taxes on the money they earn by making a profit from their enterprise, business, corporation, clothing store, etc. It doesn't take much to start an enterprise that makes a profit.

For example, I teach kids how to have two bicycles—one to ride and one to rent. How long does it take to make this simple idea work? How long does it take to make a profit? With just a little ingenuity, you're on your way in a short period of time. Remember, profits are better than wages.

Capitalism is better than communism. Communism says, "People are too stupid to know what to do with capital. You must take capital away from all the dumb, stupid people and give it to the all-wise, all-knowing state (government), and let the state run everything."

Communism has devastated every country it has touched. I've been to what was East Germany; it took a trillion dollars just to clean it up. Every country communism has touched—and I've been in all of them—has been devastated economically, socially, and especially regarding individual freedoms. It's a devastating philosophy.

We teach capital belongs in the hands of the people. That's where the ingenuity is to bring goods and services to the marketplace. Ours is an incredible philosophy that opens the doors to innovation and free-market opportunity.

## FULL-TIME, PART-TIME

When I was first recruited as a distributor for a product called Abundavita, my mentor, Mr. Shoaff, said, "Mr. Rohn, you can start this miracle-working business part-time. If you're willing to start with 10, 12, or 15 hours a week, you'll start making a profit. Then you can say, 'I'm working full-time on my job and part-time on my fortune,' because profits lead to fortune." I got so excited about that philosophy!

I found a way not only to make a living—but also to make a fortune. Can you imagine my excitement every morning to get up and go to work on my fortune? Not to go to work just to pay the rent, which is okay, but a chance to go to work to make a fortune. I thought, *Right now, I'm working part-time on my fortune and full-time on my job, but it won't be long until I'll be working full-time on my fortune! I can only imagine what life is going to be like!*

So that was my first goal when I started—I wanted to equal my profits part-time what I was earning in my full-time job.

This is called the good fortune of part-time. It was thrilling for me and the other people to start working in the business part-time because our work resulted in profits rather quickly. When I really concentrated on those 10, 12, 15 hours a week, it didn't take long.

If you really do it right and learn some of the skills you're going to read about, it won't be long until you can earn as much part-time working on your fortune as you are full-time working on your job. I did that in less than six months.

# Key phrase: It's not what happens that determines your future…

My second goal was to *make twice as much money part-time working on my fortune as I was working full-time on my job*—and I reached that in less than a year. Making twice as much money part-time, working on my fortune, as I was full-time working on my job.

When I started making twice as much money, I didn't want to quit my full-time job. Why? Because I didn't want to give up my electrifying story. It was so powerful nobody could resist the invitation to at least take a look at the opportunity for themselves. I didn't want to give it up. I hung on for so long that it was almost insane.

Then finally, finally, reluctantly, I gave up my full-time job. And now you can imagine my thrill and excitement of going to work full-time on my fortune. It was incredible.

The next philosophy that helped change my life: *It's not what happens that determines your life's future—it's what you **do** about what happens.*

We are all like little sailboats in that it's not the blowing of the wind that determines our destination, it's the set of

# ...it's what you DO about what happens.

the sail. The same wind blows on us all. The wind of disaster, the wind of opportunity, the wind of change. The wind is the same when it's favorable and unfavorable. All the economic wind, the social wind, the political wind, the same wind blows on everybody.

The difference in where you arrive in one year, three years, or five years is not the blowing of the wind but the set of the sail. That's what learning is all about, to set a better sail this year than last year. We must learn to set a better sail for the future.

The first six years of my economic life, I wound up broke. The second six years, I wound up rich. You say, "Well, the other political party must finally have the power." No, no, no. It was not a political change. What changed the second six years of my economic life was my philosophy. I set the sail for better thinking, corrected the errors of the past, and picked up new disciplines for the future. That's all I had to do at the end of the first six years—and my total life changed.

The second six years were totally different from the first six of my working life. Guess who can do that? Anybody. But if you keep on the same path for the next couple of years as you have in the past, there will be no change, none. But if you wish to or need to make some changes, I'm telling you, you can start doing it today—and the next two years will be drastically different from the last two. Anybody who wishes to do that, can. You can do it between ages 40 and 43. You can do it between ages 13 and 50. You can do it between ages 60 and 72.

Any two years, any five years that you wish to drastically change from the previous five, you can do. Now, this isn't written. This is not a law. It's called opportunity. You can change your lifestyle. You can drastically change your income, change your future, change your health, change your marriage, change everything.

Most people go year after year after year after year in the sameness as yesterday. They are not making changes simply because they don't go to class, never read a book, never went to the seminar—they never made the discovery or sought the knowledge of how to make life better.

If you just want to rock along, it's okay. Anybody can live any way they choose. But I'm here to tell you that it's possible to make the next three years totally different from the last three. All you have to do is adopt a few new philosophies. The first one is to realize that it's not the blowing of the wind that determines your income or your fortune. It's the set of the sail.

## WHAT HAPPENS, HAPPENS TO EVERYONE

I have some ideas that will help you with setting the sail of your thinking that might drastically give you multiplied more benefits in the next three years than in the last three. It's not what happens; what happens, happens to everybody.

Chevron, years ago, brought me in to talk to management. They said, "Mr. Rohn, you travel around the world and you're knowledgeable. What do you think the next ten years are going to be like?"

I said, "Gentlemen, I can tell you. I do know the right people."

They all lean forward and listen carefully.

I said, "Gentlemen, the next ten years are going to be about the last ten."

The next season after fall is...winter. I promise you that's not going to change. And after day comes? Night. I promise you that's not going to change. So my prediction of what the next ten years are going to be like is: opportunity mixed with difficulty, which has been the same for the past many centuries. Sometimes, there seems to be more opportunity than difficulty, and then sometimes, there seems to be more difficulty than opportunity—but the mix isn't going to change.

For example, after expansion comes recession, and after recession comes expansion. Not to think so is naive. Once you get these realities settled in your mind, then you know exactly what to do to anticipate so you can be ready for whatever comes along.

# Key phrase:
# For things to change, you have to change.

I was hoping the government would change and taxes would change and economics would change and my boss would change and be more generous. I wished for everything to change and my teacher said, "No, Mr. Rohn, *for things to change for you, you have to change. Don't wish it was easier; wish you were better."* Once I understood this truth, it altered the course of my life.

Don't wish life was easier—wish you were better. Here's the big one: don't wish for less problems, wish for more skills. Don't wish for less challenges, wish for more wisdom. Accept the challenges; you can't grow without challenges. You can't get rich without a challenge. You can't fly without gravity. You have to understand the challenge, which is the key to developing wisdom to overcome the challenge. Don't wish for less challenge but more wisdom.

Another philosophy that helped change my life forever: *You can do the most remarkable things no matter what happens.* Humans can do the remarkable, no matter what happens.

To complete your life-changing recipe, there are a few other critical ingredients that can make the difference: curiosity, a remarkable attitudinal quality, and two heartfelt questions.

Curiosity, wanting to know starts early in life, and it's a good quality to keep going during your lifetime; be curious about what's happening. Be curious about human beings, curious about their motives, curious about human behavior. Be curious about yourself. Be curious about government, politics, society, banking, money, the Army, the Navy, taxes, and what makes things work. What makes a city work? What makes a government work? I remember years ago, someone mentioned Russia might conquer China. I said, "If Russia conquered China, what the heck would they do with it?" Try to comprehend how the world works.

# Key phrase: Try to comprehend how the world works.

I remember going to Manhattan for the first time. I was awestruck by this huge city. Questions flooded my mind: *How does this city work? How does everything get in? How does everything get out? How does everybody get fed?* When I had a salad at lunch, the lettuce was fresh. I thought, *How does this happen?* It's a miracle how the city works. It's a miracle how the country works. How does an economy work? That a city that size stays on a steady course is amazing. Being curious is a good thing, right?

If you keep being curious, it leads to being curious about your relationships with the other people sitting at the conference table. Be curious about how you could get into the inner circle where they talk about incredible things that affect business, commerce, society, and the world.

I think the number one ingredient is curiosity. Tony Robbins attended my seminars; his attitude was an incredible, insatiable appetite for learning, which is part of curiosity. Tony went on to become a multimillionaire and involved in more than 100 businesses with combined sales of more than $7 billion annually.[1]

Being successful means you want to know. Reading books is part of that. Researching and attending class and taking notes are too.

Another ingredient is to immediately put the result of your curiosity, your knowledge, into action. Not to wait until you know it all, but to do what you know now and let the rest unfold and be revealed along the way. As an illustration... on a foggy night, if you can only see 100 feet in front of you and if you walk that 100 feet, now you can see another 100 feet. Take life in steps, a bit at a time.

These four recipe ingredients will start you on the road to success:

1. Curiosity

2. Appetite for learning

3. Willingness to put your newfound knowledge to work

4. Willingness to take constructive criticism

It's best to be open to someone's advice. For example, if someone says, "If you added this statement in your presentation, I believe it would make you twice as powerful." The best response to that constructive critic would be, "Wow, I'll consider that. Thanks." On the other hand, when you want to offer advice, there are good ways and there are blundering ways. First, give people credit for what they're already doing well, which will motivate them. Then add a few refinement suggestions. That's it. People are willing to accept that kind of constructive analysis.

Two more ingredients in my recipe are to ask two good, vital questions that get to the bottom of what makes people tick, so to speak. Number one: What turns you on? Number two: What turns you off? Two excellent questions that are food for thought.

Years ago, shortly after I met my mentor Earl Shoaff, I found out what had me turned off and I got that cured. Then I found enough reasons to get turned on, and from that day until this, no one has ever said to me, "When are you going to get going? When are you going to get off the couch? When are you going to get started?" I haven't heard those questions since I was 25 years old.

Once the fires were lit for me, they've never gone out. I've gone through my challenges from rich to broke and back to rich; I've been through it all, but no one has said, "You have to get up from here and get going."

When you are face to face with the day that turns your life around, it's one of the great experiences of a lifetime. Accumulate enough reasons to turn you on—and then just keep adding more. When you do, you will always have enough emotional and physical vitality and spiritual strength to keep going to make your life as good as possible. You will go as far as possible and earn as much as you can.

# Key phrase: Make your life as good as possible.

You will share as much as you can and be as much as you can to the people you love and care about. You will live as well as you can. When you develop that thirst and the zest for the best, you will want more for yourself and for your family.

When you know what turns you off, cut loose from that stuff. Maybe it's a negative attitude; maybe it's poor thinking. Maybe it's doomsday thinking, *The whole world is going to the dogs anyway. Why try?* If that's your mindset, I recommend listening to a good sermon or lyrics of an uplifting song or perhaps having a conversation with someone you trust who can help you turn around a negative attitude.

Remember, everyone can. Not everyone will, but everyone can—and there's no reason why you can't.

## NOTE

1. As of September 2023; see Tony Robbins's website: https://www .tonyrobbins.com/?cjdata=MXxOfDB8WXww&AID=12703194&PID= 100357191&cjevent=d0463dbb5bb311ee816a3ad50a82b832; accessed September 25, 2023.

# 3

# LIFE IN THE BALANCE

One of the biggest mistakes people make as they begin a new program of changing any aspect of their lives is moving forward too fast without sufficient forethought. It's similar to trying to drive to a destination by getting in your car and speeding away with no map to guide you. If you're not careful, you'll end up nowhere fast.

Helping you avoid making this critical mistake is what this book is all about. Ultimately, if you want to change your life for the better, you must give careful consideration to all of your values and assure preservation of each as you pursue your goals. In other words, consciously make a life, not just a living.

Earl Shoaff shared with me new ideas that were life-changing, including:

- Profits are better than wages. That statement helped me become wealthy.

- Work harder on yourself than you do on your job. I'd never heard that before.

- Success is something you attract by becoming an attractive person. It's not something you pursue.

Wow, those ideas really revolutionized my life, and I got so excited about becoming successful. I knew then I was going to become wealthy and successful, but I think I was a bit over-ambitious. Some of what I went for in the beginning cost me too much. If I'd have known what it was going to cost, I wouldn't have paid.

Sometimes, when I finally acquired "it" or reached "that" position, I looked back and said, "Wow, I spent too much time, too much money. I let go of some important values. I forgot about or misjudged what it was going to cost." So now, I always look into the future and say, "What do I really want, or need, and what is it going to cost?"

## BEHOLD AND BEWARE

There are two great words of antiquity everybody should learn—behold and beware. One is positive and one is negative. Behold is positive; beware is negative.

# Key phrases: Behold the possibilities and opportunities.

**Behold** means to gaze upon, to observe, call attention to. Behold the possibilities, behold the opportunity, behold the future and give it design. Behold all the chances you have for wealth and happiness. Behold, spring has come, the sun is shining and cold shadows are fleeing. Behold, the next person you meet might be your friend for life. Behold, the next person you talk to might be a colleague forever. *Behold* is a positive word filled with future possibilities and opportunities.

**Beware** means to be wary of, be on your guard. Beware of what you become in pursuit of what you want. Beware of a negative attitude that taints your relationships. Beware of falsehoods. Beware of hidden deceit. Beware is a negative word filled with hindering future possibilities and opportunities.

# Beware of what you become in pursuit of what you want.

# Key phrase: Behold the opportunities and beware of the dangers.

All of our lives we have to deal with behold and beware situations—behold the opportunities and beware of the dangers.

Some things I went for in the very beginning cost me too much. I got so obsessed that I found out only later that the price was too large to pay. If I would've known, I never would've paid. But sometimes we learn when? After the damage is done. So I caution you to beware; don't become so obsessed that you lose your sense of reason or it costs you family or friends. Don't be so obsessed that you compromise your virtues and your values.

The story says Judas got the money. Is that a success story? No, no. It's true, 30 pieces of silver was a sizable sum of money, but the cost was too high in the end. His guilt and shame led him to commit suicide. The greatest source of unhappiness stems from the inside. A mild form of unhappiness is constructive and inevitable. The desperate form of unhappiness is destructive. It's similar to worry. We should all worry a little but not let it destroy our lives.

If you're in New York about to step off the curb in downtown Manhattan and a taxi is approaching, it's best you worry. Worry enough to back up onto the sidewalk lest you get run over. Be cautious, not overly fearful and worrisome that it kills you, not the worry that destroys you. Worry is like hate. You don't need to hate your job. Save your hate for the important issues like the evil of betrayal, like the diabolical schemes to entice your children, and the like. You don't need to hate everything saying, "I hate this. I hate that." That's the misuse of your hate. Save it for what we really must hate.

Judas became so desperate he hung himself for what he did. He became a traitor. If Judas could speak to us he might say, "Beware of what you become in pursuit of what you want. Don't sell out. It's not worth it."

## WHOLLY BALANCED

The wholly balanced life is important. As true for adults and children, we need a balance between work and play and learning and resting. This is as true for an entrepreneur as a sales career—a doctor, as a farmer, as a pastor. Whatever your career, it is important, vital even, to find that balance of working hard so that the job gets done, but also taking the time to rest and refresh.

I used to work hard and think, *Wow, I should make time to take my family to the beach and relax.* Then I'd take my family to the beach, and at the beach, I'm thinking, *Wow, I should be at work at the office.* You have to learn to say, "When I'm at the office, I'll do office stuff. When I'm at the beach, I'll do family stuff." Balance is important in all aspects of life.

It's important to maintain good health, right? The subject of diets has had many extremes. Over the years there have been high-protein diets, low-carb diets, They had this diet that said, "High carbohydrates is the way to go," right? Sure enough, it wasn't. Now it's all finally turned around and we know a lot more, and it's called high protein, low carbohydrate, appetite suppressants, green tea diets, and all the rest. Be a student, not necessarily a follower. Read books written by reputable experts on nutrition. One may say, "If you do this, you'll live forever." The second book may say, "If you do what so-and-so says in the first book, you'll die young." So your question is, "What should I do? Which book should I follow?" I say, "Read several and then make up your own mind. You know your body better than anyone else." Be a student, not a follower.

## SELF-INTEREST

The best way I can care for you is to care for myself. The best gift I can give you is the gift of my personal development. If I become 10 times wiser, 10 times stronger, and 10 times more capable, think of what that will do for our friendship.

The first self-interest intent is to survive. I have an interesting take on the instructions given to the first couple, Adam and Eve, after the garden experience. The first instruction is to multiply. The second instruction says to be fruitful or productive; I take that to mean we need to produce enough to survive. If a man is by himself and he produces enough for himself, that's called self-care. Then if he wants to live a higher life with a companion or get married, he now must produce enough for himself and his wife.

Somebody says, "Well, why work that hard when you could just take care of yourself?" That's okay. This is not a moral question. This is a question of do you wish to live a higher life, a better life? And almost everyone would agree that a better life is to be with a companion.

But now comes the challenge to produce enough for two instead of one. Then they decide to have children. Now the man must figure out how to produce enough for himself and his family—his wife and his children. And the question always is, why do that? Why not just take care of himself? I said, this is self-care. First to survive, then to live a better life. He pays that extra price of producing more than he needs for himself so he can live a better life. Then the next challenge; is that the end of it? And the answer is no.

# Key phrase: To be generous is living an even higher life.

Why wouldn't a man think of ways now to produce more than he needs for himself and his family? To live a higher life. But why work that hard? Why do that? The answer—to be generous, which is an even higher life.

Then I take it another step further. Why not accept the challenge to produce much more than you need for yourself and for your family? Somebody says, "Well, that's ridiculous. Why do that?" Answer: to live a higher life.

Then I take it one step further. Why not produce far more than you need? What a way to live! Extraordinary! Providing for others is the highest form of living. It's okay to live an ordinary life and a pretty good life, but how about an extraordinary life, to produce far more than you need for yourself and your children?

Suppose you make $10 million a year, and you and your family only need $3 million to live comfortably. Now you have $7 million to give, to share with others. How about that kind of life? It's called extraordinary—to produce more and far more than you need for yourself.

## HIGH-QUALITY LIFESTYLE

How wonderful it is to get joy from your substance and be able to share that joy with others. A life that is aligned with values does not have to be dull and boring. Quite to the contrary, the art of living well can be developed in almost any circumstance to expand your celebration of all that life has to offer.

It's best to enjoy some of that early money in lifestyle changes. Go to the movies, take two vacations instead of one.

Just some little extras so the family gets inspired by this new commitment to earning more and becoming more. And taking the time to study and learn the skills, whatever you have to do to make it more worthwhile for the family by thinking of and appreciating the exciting lifestyle changes. Go to a concert.

My parents said, "Don't miss anything. Don't miss the play, the music, the songs, the performances, the movie, whatever's happening." At age 93, my father, before he died, if you would've called him at 10:30 or 11 o'clock at night, he wouldn't be home. He'd be at the rodeo, at church, at the play, a performance. During the day, he'd be watching the kids play softball, all at age 93. So he did it as well as taught it. Don't miss anything. Make those changes in your lifestyle.

When I started making some extra money, I opened a bank account for my wife and called it "No Questions Asked Account." As a stay-at-home mom, I told her, "I'll keep putting money in there and you spend it for whatever you wish." It was life-changing for her. She no longer had to ask me for money because I could sense that it was a little embarrassing at times. You can't believe what that did for her self-esteem and our marriage. It was absolutely amazing; these changes in lifestyle affect everyone in the family. It's called making a living but also making a life.

## THE GOOD LIFE

Lifestyle, social friendships, church, community, country—all make a composite of our overall life. Start furnishing that with new vigor, vitality, money, whatever it takes to expand your life into what I call *the good life,* as well as economics. It doesn't take a lot. How much is a movie? Even for a person of modest means, $6 or $10? It costs $60 million to make it and only costs $6 to see it. Part of it's just simply priority. Fewer soft drinks and popcorn, more movies. Everybody's got money. There's a story I tell of the lady who invested the dollar she had—and now she's a millionaire. She had the dollar. How your story ends depends on where you put your dollar.

I now routinely have four-hour lunches with my grand-children who are now 15 and 16, talking about everything. We sit out on the veranda at the La Playa Hotel in Carmel, overlooking the ocean and the gardens. After our four-hour lunches, I'm so much richer than when I sat down in terms of exchanging ideas, confidences, experiences, plans for the future, accomplishments—it's exciting! There is probably nothing more rewarding than a conversation with those you love and colleagues as well.

Although, too, sometimes you need to be alone. For all of my busy life, from Milan to New York, to Paris, to Mexico City, to the giant cities of the world, I do seek solitude, but only for short periods of time, not long periods of time. But it is important for me to get away, think and ponder and wonder about my life and what's happening, what's going on, where to go from here.

But some of the greatest rewards are in personal conversation. I have some close friends, some mentors who have been around for the past 50 years for me. A couple of hours of conversation and I have enough to feast on and live on until we meet again.

# Key phrase: Living well doesn't cost a fortune— all it costs is paying attention.

Sometimes, it's easy to be a little too busy to go to lunch with a close friend or spend an evening with family members and enjoy life. How much is a concert ticket? $25, $30, $40? Somebody says, "Well, poor people can't afford to go to a concert." I say, "No, it costs only about eight Coca-Colas." It just depends on where you spend the money you have. So you save up your soft drink money and then go and do something special. The lifestyle to live well doesn't cost a fortune. All it costs is paying attention.

## THE VERY BEST SIDE OF LIFE

Then the little dramas. I tell the story about calling my father after my mother died. My father lived another eight years. He spent one more year on the farm, which I still have in Idaho, where I make a little wine and grow a few crops and live the good life overlooking the Snake River. My father spent one more year there, but during the nights, he was a little lonely. So I got him a place in the little farm village close by where he could go and spend the night, have breakfast, and then jump in his car and go back to the farm.

The Decoy Inn is a little cafe where my father, almost every morning, would have breakfast with the farmers. So I'd call him there and they'd bring the phone to him at the table. "Papa, I'm in Israel," and we'd have a conversation and he'd talk real loud so they could all hear the details. "They gave me a reception last night on the rooftop," he'd say. "Underneath the stars, pop?" He'd say, "Underneath the stars."

Everybody gets in on this little conversation he's having with me, and now he has a story to tell for the rest of the day. "My son called me from Israel and I know he had to get up in the middle of the night...." It made a much more special day for him—and it only took 10 minutes out of my day to make his better. Easy, too easy not to. There are dozens of ways you can make someone's day better, too.

I'd send my father postcards from around the world and he'd save them, show them around. When I'd return and visit him, some of the postcards had a little butter and jelly on them from passing them around at breakfast. And then he'd get to retell the story. "I was showing these postcards to my friends and here's what happened and here's what they said..." And it keeps this lively interchange between father and son going.

One year, I took my father back to where he was born, Odessa, Washington. We went to the newspaper office in this little community and he found some newspapers dated 1903, the year he was born. There was no record of his birth. I said,

"You were born out in the country, Papa, no record of your birth here." Then we went back to where he last attended school. He told me that he used to arrive early before the teachers got there and lit the fires in an old stove in the one- or two-room school. But it was gone now. Tried to locate the place where he lived and couldn't find it either.

The only buildings left that my dad recognized was a church and a bar. He looked at me and said, "Well, that's a pretty good combination, get messed up in one place and get straight- ened out in the other." I said, "That's good, Papa." To keep that kind of relationship alive, my parents were extraordinary and the little things you can think of that makes lifestyle unique. It's not a matter of cost, it's really more a matter of time than cost.

In the process of consciously changing any area of your life and creating the life you want—you will get great enjoyment when you appeal to the very best side of your nature.

Everybody has a different temperament and personality that is developed over a period of time. If you're too shy, it's best to push that side of you into a small corner—and speak up more. If you're a little too loud, try to calm down just a little bit. But don't try to just radically become someone else.

To be civil in a civil society, we must deal with the dark side of our nature and expose the positive side of our nature. It isn't that that process ever gets done or finished, but we should suppress what causes us trouble, not only within ourselves, but causes us trouble with someone else. This is a never-end- ing challenge, but it is worth the effort. We could describe we humans as having a dual nature—and the key to life is to become the most of the good in us and the least of the bad.

# Key phrase:
# Strive to become the most of the good in you and the least of the bad.

It's so important also to work on what is not in your best interest, both in your thinking process and developing your plans for the future, in your process of working with others, sitting at a conference table, or being involved in an enterprise. Those are constants in life. When some become wealthy, they have to deal with an ego that didn't show its ugly head until the money was flowing. Now this little gremlin on one shoulder whispers, "Now's the time to conquer the world and let everybody know you're the master." And sure enough, it can cause all kinds of problems.

In the next chapter, we'll work on getting rid of that little gremlin.

# 4

# YOUR NATURE'S POSITIVE SIDE

One of the greatest difficulties of wealth is handling this issue of ego and keeping it under control. Although we need to reveal who we are, we also need to master the art of presenting our best selves, as it serves us and our children, as it serves us and our friends, as it serves us and our business. This is a constant aspect of life that never ends.

We can make a personal appeal to ourselves, "I want to constantly work on developing the positive side of my nature and do my best to suppress the darker side that prevents me from being the most of what I can possibly be." I think that is what's important.

When leaders in any position elevate themselves because of an overactive ego, the power they wield becomes detrimental to everyone. There have always been good leaders and bad leaders. Whether a good king, bad king, or whether inside our own head, we all have to deal with ego. But we might make this note: it's all part of the great adventure to deal with it, to become civilized and not allow ourselves as we journey along to become uncivilized in our behavior, in our language, in our style, and to try to keep that balance going consistently and present that as the best part of us is who we are, and then let people see that.

# Key phrase: Present the best part of yourself as who you really are.

Part of creating a life worth living is pursuing a job or career that you have always dreamed about. Some authors call this pursuing your passion. Yet I believe that the constant obsession with your passion can distract you from beginning your success journey. Better to start right where you are and let your passion find you.

I think trying to find your passion is a bit too strong a word. Greatly desiring to be extremely successful is probably sufficient. But if you can find something you really love to do and can do it with great passion, I think that's fantastic.

Yet, I think being grateful is number one. If you have a job, be grateful and say, "This isn't the greatest job in the world," but even if it's a transitional job getting you where you want to go, be grateful. You don't have to love your job or be passionate about your job. Just passionate about staying steady, working hard, learning skills, and doing this job so well that the next one will be even better. Taking such good care of this opportunity, another one will present itself.

Sometimes people say, "Well, if I had a good job, I'd really pour it on, but I've got this lousy job, so I just goof off." That's *not* the attitude nor the philosophy that attracts a successful future. Even though it may not be the best job in the world, if it furnishes a living, you have to be grateful. If it takes care of you and your family, you have to have gratitude. Not necessarily passion for the job but gratitude for it.

If you have an extreme desire to be successful so you can accomplish all you wish to accomplish, be as generous as you'd like to be, be as strong as you'd like to be in terms of financial strength, and be involved in entrepreneurial projects, go for it!

I think if you say you have to "find your passion," people find that a little bit confusing, thinking, *Where would I find it, and what could I be passionate about?* I guess you could start with saying, "I'm passionate about providing unusual success for myself and for my family so that my children will say in the years to come, 'We had the most incredible life together as a family.'" Then if that is the case, I think the key is to let what you want to accomplish grow.

Where at first this is as far as you can see, you can then say, "Wow, maybe I can multiply by two, by three and expand my vision, accomplish a lot more." If you have an enterprise, you could take steps to make it stronger and better, more far-reaching. Let that happen. We can figure out the next little part of our life that we can see, and then we can say, "Well, eventually, I'd like to have..." and let those dreams linger somewhere in your consciousness until opportunities are presented, and you take advantage of each one.

## MAKE A LIST

I say make a list of all the things that would give you the most incredible life. Make that list. What would do it for you over the next 10 or 20 years? Places to go, things to see, people to meet, books to read, skills to learn, investments to make, being generous to who and what and where. I encourage you to make lists of all the things that you think would make for you a really fantastic life. And at first, don't worry about how to get everything you list. Just let your mind run free and think about what would really do it for you.

Then, realize that the lists may need to be altered over time. You may start working toward something and then think, *Sure enough, I thought this was really going to be everything I wanted, but now I can see it's not.* Long before you are going to accomplish your goal, you may realize, "I'm investing too much money and time and effort," so you wisely change direction.

And any time you want, you can tear up your whole list and start all over again. Some people may say, "I made the list so I have to accomplish everything on it." No, you don't. It's your life. It's your list. You can turn it upside down, right side up, scratch off some things, put some new things on, or start all over again. Don't let it become an obsession. Let it become an enticement. Better to be enticed than obsessed, or we might invest too much effort and time in something that's not really going to turn out to be as great as we thought it would.

# Key phrase:
# Better to be enticed than obsessed.

An old prophet said, "Sometimes things that taste good in the mouth later turn bitter in the belly." We think, *Oh, this is it!* Yet, it was a bit of an illusion. Remember the lyrics for "Don't Cry for Me, Argentina"? One of the lines is, "They are illusions; they're not the solutions they promised to be." Changing direction is a learning experience, affected by what we see.

Maybe we shouldn't have devoted so much of our time and energy pursuing a goal, but if that's what we could see at the moment, we were going to work at it and learn as we go. We need a collection of experiences to give us good data on what to do, what not to do. That's life.

Many times, you need more experience to make a wiser decision. If a person says, "Well, I've eaten junk food now for a week, but look how strong and healthy I am," that's a delusion. One week is not going to give you the right kind of information about how you feel, whether it's a good idea to continue or not. You need a lot more experience than that to decide whether or not it's good for you.

During a seminar, I used the following illustration as an example. While holding a lit candle, while talking about having enough experience to make wise decisions, I said, "Would all of you agree that the fire will burn my finger?"

"Yes, the fire will burn your finger," they respond.

So I put my finger in the flame and take it out fairly quickly, in and out, right in the flame and out. And I say, "Look, my finger's okay. Where did you get the idea that the flame would burn my finger?"

They say, "No, no, Mr. Rohn. You can't just put your finger in and out of the flame quickly to know that the flame will burn your finger. You have to leave your finger in the flame longer."

I say, "Oh, yes, then I need a little more experience to make a wise decision."

Then, to drive home the principle, I say, "Well, what about the person who says they use cocaine and feel okay." This is only the beginning when it seems to be okay; they don't know the end of that road. If they don't have any personal experience with cocaine, they need to ask someone who does. That person will tell them, "Look, 20 years of my life was wasted, and I finally turned it around. Cocaine is bad; it will ruin your life. Just look at some of those old rock and rollers who have turned it around—and the others who died."

One time, when I was in Paris presenting to a class of 20,000, also in town were the Rolling Stones, with Mick Jagger and all the rest. Some of these guys made it through those treacherous days of drugs and alcohol. A lot of them didn't make it. Boy George said, "I woke up one day, and all my friends were dead." That's enough experience.

If you haven't had enough experience and you're just getting started, it's wise to ask somebody who has been down that road for maybe four or five years or even 20. Then, you can make a good judgment based on a lot more relevant data.

## SHORT LIST FOR A GOOD LIFE

Creating a rich and fulfilling life based on your values is the way to an enjoyable lifestyle. The following section offers a short list for a good life.

### NUMBER ONE, PRODUCTIVITY.

If you don't produce, you won't be happy.

### NUMBER TWO, GOOD FRIENDS.

The greatest support system in the world is good friends. You must work on that. Don't be careless here. Friends are those wonderful people who know all about you and still like you.

### NUMBER THREE, SPIRITUALITY.

I'm not asking you to be a believer. I am a believer that humans are more than an advanced form of the animal kingdom. I'm a believer that we're a special creation. I don't ask you to be a believer, but here's what I do ask. If you are a believer, here's what you must do: study, practice, and teach. Whatever's valuable to you, study, practice, and teach. Why? It builds the foundation that builds the country, that builds the nation, that helps us to compete among the nations of the world in the 21st century. Share what you know with others.

## NUMBER FOUR, DON'T MISS OUT.

My parents taught me not to miss anything. Don't miss the game. Don't miss the performance. Don't miss the show, the movie, don't miss the words. We're all inspired by words. Elton John says, "She lived her life like a candle in the wind, never knowing who to cling to when the rain set in." Don't miss those lyrics, the music, the song that nourishes the soul. I can't describe better than that how brief and fragile life is.

George Harrison, one of The Beatles sings, "If not for you, the winter would hold no spring. Couldn't hear a robin sing. I just wouldn't have a clue if not for you." Wow. Remember the words that reflect the experience. Barbara Streisand sings, "It used to be so natural to talk about forever, but used-to-bes don't count anymore. They just lay on the floor 'til we sweep them away. You don't sing me love songs. You don't say you need me, and you don't bring me flowers anymore." Illustrative of all of our experiences.

Winston Churchill said, "The truth is incontrovertible. Malice may attack it, and ignorance made deride it, but in the end, there it is." Use that, feast on someone else's comments; you could stay up all night and not think of that statement of Churchill's. I'm asking you to do your research. I'm asking you to not miss anything. Even the small things, don't miss; the big things, don't miss. They are all part of living a good life.

Why? Each experience will serve you well forever. If you live well, you will earn well. If you live well, it'll show up in the texture of your voice. If you live well, it'll show up in your face. If you live well, it'll show up in the magnetism of your personality, if you live well. So don't miss the nourishment of all the things around you that could help you live a good life.

## NUMBER FIVE, TAKE CARE OF YOUR INNER CIRCLE.

When you take care of them, they'll take care of you. Inspire them; they will inspire you. Nothing is more valuable than your inner circle. That's where the power to conquer the world comes from—family and friends.

When a father walks out of the house and he can still all day long feel his daughter's kiss on his face, he's a powerful man. That nourishment is so incredible. If a husband walks out of the house and all day long he feels the imprint of his wife's arms around his body, he's invincible. Who can touch him? No one. One person caring for another, the old prophet said, "Is the greatest of virtues." There are many virtues and values, but the greatest is love. Better to live in a tent on the beach with someone you love than to live in a mansion by yourself. People caring for people, and especially that inner circle where the power is so magnificent that when you draw from it and you nourish it, it nourishes you.

## NUMBER SIX, ASK FOR GOD'S HELP.

We could all use a little help, but my whole seminar was about what you can do. A man took a rock pile and turned it into a fabulous garden. Somebody came and saw it and said,

"You and the good Lord have this fabulous garden here." The gardener said, "I understand your point, but you should have seen it a few years ago when God had it all by himself." So we do play a part.

# THE FOUR IFS THAT MAKE LIFE WORTHWHILE

Wrapping up this chapter on Your Nature's Positive Side, we examine what makes life worthwhile—the "ifs" of it. A message we desperately need today to turn ourselves and our world around.

## 1. LIFE IS WORTHWHILE IF YOU LEARN.

Of course, the beginning of being a civilized person, a person of accomplishment, is to learn. We learn as we go through those early grades in school. Part of the learning process starts before we go to school; we learn from our parents, mother and father, hopefully. I was very fortunate to have excellent parents who taught me well. My mother taught me how to read and write before I went to school, so it made school a lot easier, and I enjoyed it all the years I went through high school and one year of college, but my parents gave me that great extra advantage from what they taught me in those years before school. And then the rest of it is learning as you go, from school to enterprise, getting a job, learning what marriage is all about, the opportunity and responsibility, children, learning the possibilities. It's unique that the possibilities are always far more than we can imagine.

So first, we imagine the possibilities. Then, we imagine the possibilities that are possible for us, and I think we need both. Someone gives their testimonial and says, "I started with this and I became wealthy, and if I can do it, you can do it." And they take us into a story of possibilities far beyond what we think we could possibly accomplish, but at least we can take from that testimonial their comment that "If I can do it, you can do it. I started with nothing and look what happened for me. You could do it," but on our part now, it's a matter of personal choice, but at least it gives us a glimpse into the full range of possibilities.

The minimum wage income level now in the United States is $5 an hour, up to what? Top income last year was $68 million, one person earned for one year. That's the full range of possibilities. Then, we have to figure out on that full range of possibilities, what's possible for us? Then, you go as far as you can see at the moment, but accomplishment is just like ambition. Accomplishment helps you to see that much more. Once you have learned some skills and gained some experience, you learn from that and say, "Wow, maybe a couple of more skills and I could multiply my value by two, by three, by five, plus my income, plus my ability to be influential, powerful, and helpful." So it's true. Life is worthwhile if you learn.

When I lecture high school or college students, I tell them, "There's nothing worse than being stupid. Make sure you get the information while you're here in school. You can sort through it later—throw some away, forget some, whatever, but make sure you get it. Being broke is bad, but being stupid is really bad, and what's really, really bad is being broke and stupid. You have to learn. Part of it we learn by trial and error. We do it wrong and learn to do it right. We think it's right, and we work it, and it doesn't work. So now we learn from that.

Hopefully, we learn fast as quick as possible, but it's true. Life is worthwhile if you learn."

## 2. LIFE IS WORTHWHILE IF YOU TRY.

Learn something and then give it a try, see if you can do it, see if it'll work for you. We play games to see if we can win. You can't just say "win." No, you have to try. You play the best you can. We play to see if we can get a higher score than the other team. When we do, we walk off winners. But if we lose, that doesn't mean we're losers, it only means we lost the game. So the key is to try again to see if we can win next time, put a better combination together. The same is true economically or with a job or employment or enterprise.

The farmer plants in the spring, takes care of it all summer, but at harvest time, a hailstorm comes along and beats his crop into the ground, which means now all is lost in terms of his harvest. So the question is, should he ever try again? Of course! The law of averages says more often than not, if you plant in the spring, you'll have a harvest in the autumn. So of course, even if all was lost, the smart farmer will try again in the spring. Not a guarantee, but a promise and an opportunity, and that's all of us can do—try our best with whatever opportunities come our way.

Part of life is learning to recognize opportunity and take advantage of it. If you have a chance, the opportunity to meet somebody new, don't let it slip by. It could be the chance of a lifetime, an open door. Keep trying; try to learn not to miss opportunities. Then when the record book is finished on your life, let it show your wins. Let it show your losses, but don't let it show you didn't try. See what you can do. So life is worthwhile if you learn. Second, if you try.

## 3. LIFE IS WORTHWHILE IF YOU STAY.

Some people plant in the spring and leave in the summer when it gets hot. The weather's not to their liking and the weeds are too tall and the work is too hard, but you have to stay to succeed. My advice is to stay at least through the cycle. Doesn't mean you have to stay forever, but at least if you've planted in the spring, see it through to the harvest and see what comes of it. It's like going to a game, stay till it's over. I say it's good training. Even though your team is behind, if you walk out and your team is behind, it's rude. If you support your team, you probably wouldn't leave until it was over. Even if your team is hopelessly behind, that's good practice.

If you lay the foundation, at least see the project through, finish this one. Doesn't mean you have to plant or play ever again, but at least see if you can accomplish this one to stay, stay through the summer, stay through the challenges, stay until at least this project is finished and then make a decision on whether to plant again or whether to start another project or whatever again.

Probably more marriages could be saved if they decided to stay at least a little longer to see if it could be worked out. Sometimes, it might not be possible, but at least stay and try. See if there's another answer, another alternative, another way—and there usually is. So, you will have a worthwhile life if you learn, if you try, and if you stay; my last "if" is if you care.

## 4. LIFE IS WORTHWHILE IF YOU CARE.

If you care at all, you'll get results. If you care enough, you could get *incredible* results. Part of the miracle of the human capability and possibility is the ability to care, to love, to truly care about someone else, care about your family, your enterprise, your country, your community, your friendships. Care enough to repair what goes wrong, care enough to confront the challenges to make something better.

It is a great human characteristic to care about what happens to those we love and to care about what happens in the future. It is easy to be tempted not to care, especially if you're a bit of a distance from it. For instance, I made a trip last year to India, my third trip to India. Unless you see it for yourself, it's hard to comprehend a country with so much poverty and extreme challenges for the people there.

There might not be anything you can do personally except maybe offer your prayers, but you can at least care about what happens, with hope that their lives will improve. That ways and means of feeding the poor, inspiring the children, giving hope to the father who wants to take care of his family, whether it's in some remote village or some dusty New Delhi street—it's important to care about the world, which direction it's going when the world is half slave and half free. That's a difficult scenario to process, but we should at least care.

Abraham Lincoln said, "Since I would be no one's slave, I will be no one's master." That's good caring, caring put in philosophical terms. And then care about each other, especially the people you work with and you're close to because it takes everybody. One person doesn't make an economy. One person doesn't make an institution, an enterprise, a business. It takes all gifts blended together to make something work and learning to appreciate each person's value.

# Key phrase:
# Care about others; appreciate each person's value.

I said to my audience of about 1,000 people in Colorado Springs, "It took everybody being here to make this occasion. Those who invited others and spread the word. Then I walked into the seminar room. I walked in by myself, but when I walked away after the event, I carried away with me the spirit of all the people, the reaction of all the people. I had a chance to meet several people, and I walked away with their testimonial or their good wishes."

The same is true for you. When you walk into any situation, you only bring one person, but you make a contribution to the whole. So what's the big factor, the result? The multiplying factor is that the whole makes a contribution to you as an individual.

By contributing only one person, you, your handshake, your smile, your participation, your reaction, affects everyone there. And you walk away with the substance of everybody, which makes you much richer than when you walked in.

People have often asked, "What would you like people to remember about you?" My answer: I've been given so many extraordinary opportunities, and I would like to know that I've made a contribution, and if when I'm gone they say, "He made a major contribution to the lives of millions"—that'd be an extraordinary thing to say about me.

But I think as long as toward the end of your life you find yourself respected by your family and your close friends, that's probably just about as good as it gets. They know who you are, probably better than anyone else. They know your dignity. They know your service. They know your dreams. They know your commitments. They know the hard work you've done.

They know the contribution you've made better than anyone else—and if you have their respect toward the end of your life, family and close friends, whether the world recognizes it or not or sees it or not, or whether they build a statue in your honor, or fail to put your name in the Hall of Fame, it really wouldn't matter that much.

# 5

# OVERCOMING SETBACKS

**W**hile it only takes a day to turn your life around and begin walking a new road to build a successful life, you need to continue walking down the new road day in, day out. You need to continue to pay the price of success, so that you build new habit patterns of thought and action. Yet, inevitably, there will be times when you veer off the road and lose your bearings. In other words, you will encounter adversity, perhaps great adversity, on the path to success.

The key is not to avoid adversity but to learn how to redirect your efforts, reestablish your successful habits, and walk again. You certainly don't want to end up in the ditch.

As mentioned previously, I was a millionaire by age 31 and broke by age 33. Two and a half million dollars all swept away as the result of making foolish decisions. That first money I made was really hard to keep. As a young guy, I fell for some temptations.

You know that old saying, "A fool and his money are soon parted." That was me. When I saw something I liked, I'd say,

"How many colors does it come in? I'll buy them all!" That kind of recklessness was foolish. On top of that, I made some unwise business decisions.

A company wanted to borrow a quarter of a million dollars and the bank said, "Well, if Mr. Rohn will sign personally, we'll let you have the money." I knew they could pay it back, so I signed, so I'm the hero. They paid it back, but I find out a little bit later that the company was in financial trouble and went back to the bank to borrow another quarter of a million. I said to myself, "Well, I hope they don't call me because this time I won't sign." I signed the first note, and it was all paid back, but I knew they weren't going to make it this time, and they never called about me signing the second note.

However, sure enough, within a year the company goes belly up. Then, I get a letter from the bank saying, "Dear Mr. Rohn, we have here your guarantee that if the company can't perform, you will make good on the quarter of a million that was borrowed from our bank. Please send us your check."

I called the bank and said, "Hey, there's been some mistake here. I signed the first note, but nobody ever called me about another note. I never signed the second note."

What I didn't know was that the note I had originally signed was a "continuing guarantee." I knew right then what the word "continuing" meant. I knew how much it cost per letter.

But anyway, that and a few other "learning experiences" and my newfound wealth disappeared. So sure enough, from poor to rich and from rich back to poor, what do I do now?

## MORE VALUABLE THAN MONEY

What occurred to me was that even though my money was gone, I still had the skills—and the skills proved to be more valuable than the money. So I just simply went back to work, went back to the street, went back using the formula I had used in the first place to do well, and made many times more what I did the first time.

That's the key! You have to go back to work, and part of that realization was that I had to be willing to readjust my lifestyle. The fancy cars had to go, the homes and all that stuff had to go. I went back to a modest apartment and a modest place and pulled everything down to start over rather than try and keep living a lifestyle I couldn't afford.

When you have to start over, return to whatever you have to do. Put it all back together again, no different from the farmer who plants in the spring and when a hailstorm destroys the crop, he goes back in the spring and says, "Let's try it one more time."

Once in a while you may get wiped out two years in a row but not that often. So you try it again. And probably from the experience, if you treat it right and keep the right attitude, you'll be stronger than you were the first time around or the second time around.

When I first started working on my fortune as well as my living, my mentor said, "Life depends on your attitude." If you say, "I'm working a little extra time to pay some bills," that'd be one thing, but if you say, "I'm working a little extra time to start my fortune," that makes getting out of bed totally different. To get up to pay some extra bills is one thing. To get up to lay the foundation for your fortune is a whole different attitude and mindset and philosophy.

# Key phrase: Everything comes down to attitude and philosophy.

So if you have the right attitude, no matter what has happened, if you readjust your attitude, philosophy, and adopt a whole new positive mindset, you can start again and be successful. Some great fortunes are made after a person turns 50 or 60 years old. Why? Because with all the ups and downs that happened to them in those accumulation of years, now when an idea or a new burst of energy or vitality or goal sets in, they have all their past experiences to invest. That's why incredible fortunes have been made even after age 50 or even 60.

When you're 20 years old, you don't have much experience to invest. It doesn't mean you can't do okay and climb the ladder fairly quickly, though—many have. But when you're

30, you have a bit more experience to invest and are better equipped to bounce back if something happens and you have to start over. But sure enough, at 50 or 60, you have a good handful of years of experience to invest, which may make all the difference in the world.

And it's true that you can tip either way when you face a setback—you can be discouraged by it all, or you can be inspired by it all. And that's part of the mystery of life. It's up to you to turn around, try again, and make another fortune. The mystery is not everybody will do that. Some will use setbacks as a reason to succeed. Others use it as a reason to give up. Same circumstances.

A study was done in which they followed two boys, twins. The father of these two boys was a scoundrel and a drunk. Years later, one of the twins turned out to be a scoundrel and a drunk. He was asked, "Why did your life turn out like this?"

He said, "Well, what would you expect? My father was a scoundrel and a drunk. What else would you expect?"

The other twin turned out to be a professional doing very well. And he was asked, "How did you turn out to be a professional?"

He said, "I didn't want to be like my father."

Same father, yet one son used it as an excuse for living a less-than-enjoyable life. And the other son used it as a reason to make all the necessary changes to live a good life.

## ASSOCIATIONS

A big share of your life, a majority of your life, is shaped by attitude and by influence, which includes the people around you. Good questions to ask yourself:

- Who are the people I am around most?
- What influence do they have on me?
- Am I okay with how they influence me?

Other good questions to ask yourself:

- What do they read?
- Where do they go?
- What do they do?
- How do they think and behave?
- Is that what I want to read, where I want to go, what I want do to, think, and behave?

Taking these questions seriously and answering each one will give you a good mature analysis of your life right now. If your answer is that you're okay with the answers, fine. If you're not okay, make some positive changes.

Association can make all the difference in the world in your future. It's best to practice limited association. Some people you can be around a few hours but not a few days. And some people you can be around a few minutes but not a few hours. And then some people you have to walk away and leave behind.

## CLOSER THAN A BROTHER

Sometimes, it's helpful if somebody comes along and helps us in a moment of stress and distress and offers a book or some advice. They just say, "I'll be here when you need me." Sometimes, that's enough. Having a few good friends who will be there if you need them, that's valuable.

I lost a friend just a few years ago, David. I used to say of David, if I was stuck in a foreign jail accused unduly somewhere, if they allowed me one call, I would call him. And the reason is, he would come and get me, no questions asked. That's what I call a real friend.

Hopefully, in times of stress or if you've fallen out of the tech sky and the paper's all burned up and the money's all gone and the project turned into reverse. Hopefully, you have some friends or a friend around who can give you the support you need to make it through the rough patches.

I encourage you to make the kind of friends on your way up who will be there on your way down. Someone who will kindly say, "Come in. I've been expecting you. The way you were going, I knew it wouldn't be long until the bubble would burst and everything would go in reverse. Come on in, let's talk things over."

So make some good friends, so that no matter what happens, when things turn upside down, you have a few friends to rely on for wise counsel. I've had some of those great friends in my life. They helped save my life, save my career, save everything. Walk the beach or sit with a cup of coffee with somebody who cares about you and is an excellent friend. Where you can really unload and sort it out with someone who sincerely cares about you.

Sometimes a business venture that goes wrong is like being in a car wreck. It takes a while for your mind to clear. If you've been in a wreck or are in the midst of one now and you're out there kind of wandering around, sometimes it's helpful if somebody takes you by the hand and says, "Hey, let's sit down here for a while until your mind stops spinning." There's no way to put a value on that, how valuable that is.

## RECOVER QUICKLY

Adversity separates the pro and the amateur, be it in sports, business, or life. The key is to not avoid adversity but recover quickly.

# Key phrase: Recover quickly from adversity.

The amateur loses a close game and is probably affected for a long time. Or on the golf course makes a poor shot, which affects the rest of his play. But when a pro like Tiger Woods makes a poor shot, he knows he has to settle in and not let that one affect the next one. That's the difference between an amateur and a pro.

When the amateur loses a close game, it may affect him forever. When the pro loses a close game, he is affected too. Don't get between him and the locker door—he'll put a dent in you. He's angry and upset, but it doesn't last long. A few hours later, after a shower and something to eat, he's saying, "Tomorrow night we'll run them off the court. Not next year, tomorrow night!"

So the key to a quick recovery is to have something to go for right away. "I'll really work on my jump shot and the next game we'll win!" Or "I'll put a new project together within the next 90 days." Or "My presentation next week will be a show-stopper!" Instead of letting a setback affect you for a year or a couple of years, put something together quickly. It may not be the total answer, but it's the answer for now to get you to overcome a setback.

One of the greatest things I learned in my studies with Earl Shoaff is that life does not give us what we need. Life gives us what we deserve. You don't reap a harvest because you need it. You reap a harvest because you deserve it. You planted in the spring and took care of it in the summer.

One of the ways to help a mother on welfare, the person comes with the welfare check. But now, with better information, she says to Mary, "Mary, the next time I come with the welfare check for you and your children, here's a bucket of paint and a paintbrush. And if these posts are painted, and if the front door is painted, the next time I come back next month, you get the money." This is a starting point for the mother to gain the sense of not getting something because she needs it but getting something because she deserves it. Not that painting the two posts and the door deserves $500, but it's a start.

# Key phrase:
# Life doesn't give you what you need, life gives you what you deserve.

Then the next time, the welfare lady says, "If this fence is painted and if these weeds are gone and if these flowers are planted the next time I come, you get the $500 again."

This process is starting to walk Mary from her desperate situation into a mode and philosophy and thinking of "What else could I do to deserve more money?" It's the whole difference in trying to get something because you need it rather than getting something because you deserve it. "How can I learn to deserve it?"

My daughter may say, "I need $10."

No answer.

"I have to have $10 for school tomorrow."

No answer.

Then she remembers, "Daddy, how could I earn $10?"

Response, "Here's how you can earn $10."

This family has plenty of money. I mean the vaults here are full, but the key to unlock the vault is not to get something because you need it but to get something because you deserve it.

This is great life training for kids, a mother on welfare, whoever. How can I begin the process of deserving? That's what Mr. Shoaff called personal development.

As mentioned previously, but worth stating again, learning new strategies is like the sailboat. The wind blows on every sailboat, but the difference in destination is the set of the sail, not the blowing of the wind. Some winds are contrary, some are severe, some are easy, some are gentle. So the same wind blows on us all. The difference in where we arrive three years from now is not the blowing of the wind, it's the set of the sail. Philosophy, attitude, willingness to do the basics and fundamentals to make a new start.

## DISCIPLINING YOUR DISAPPOINTMENT

There's an amazing law that contains the perfect recipe for practicing the art of disciplining your disappointment—the law of sowing and reaping, a great philosophical framework to fall back on when times get tough.

The law of sowing and reaping is also the story of the law of averages, which we talked about briefly in Chapter 2. The story of the sower comes from the Bible. I'm an amateur on the Bible, but this is such a useful story and the drama's in the details.

The sower was ambitious and had excellent seed. The excellent seed can be an excellent opportunity, an excellent product, an excellent story. So we've got an ambitious sower with excellent seed.

First, the sower goes out to sow the seed, but the first part of the seed falls by the wayside and the birds get it. Likewise, the birds are going to get some of your seed.

You may say, "Mr. Rohn, what does that mean?"

Well, suppose I invite John to come to a meeting and he said he'd be there Tuesday night. Tuesday night I show up, and John isn't there. *I wonder why John didn't make it.* I know the answer. The birds. John had the great idea of coming to the meeting to look at an opportunity and somebody stole it by saying with a sneer, "You're not going to that network marketing meeting, are you?"

And John says, "Well, maybe not."

So you have to realize that the birds are going to get some of your excellent seed that you sow. Now, when the birds get some, you have two options. Number one is to chase the birds, thinking you'll tell that other person he should mind his own business. But I recommend that you not do this. If you go off chasing birds, you leave the field, which is going to distract from your future, not add. So you can't chase birds and try to straighten this stuff out.

The second option is to acknowledge it for what it is—just one of those things. The best comment when things are a little disappointing is to say, "Isn't that interesting? I thought for sure John would be there. He promised me, but I know it was the birds."

The story continues. It says the sower continued to sow. That was the secret to his success. He kept on sowing. And if you keep sowing, you can sow more than the birds can get. If you keep sowing, the law of averages will work for you.

My mentor taught me, saying, "You know Mr. Rohn, there are only nine or ten real nasty, miserable people in the whole world. They move around a lot, and you'll probably bump into one once in a while. But when you bump into one, you know there's only nine more like that one. And you can handle that!"

Okay, so now the sower keeps sowing the seed, and some falls on rocky ground where the soil is shallow. This circumstance is not of your making—you had excellent seed and you are an ambitious sower. But here's what happened. This time, the little seed that falls in the ground starts to grow, and a little plant emerges. But the first hot day, it withers and dies. Not an easy thing to watch.

Likewise, I keep sowing excellent seeds, and finally, John gets started. Yet sure enough, three or four days later, somebody says, "Boo," and he's gone. Doesn't show up at the second meeting.

*I thought sure John would last a week. What happened?* The hot weather is going to get some. And this is not of your making. Here's what you must say when that happens, "Isn't that interesting?" What can you do? The answer is nothing. Just let that happen. Don't go for this, "Why? Why? Why?" stuff.

The answers are in the structure, and the consequences, and in the deal. Anything beyond that is not worth studying.

You may ask why some participate only for a little while. Some don't stay. When some leave, all you can do is cooperate with the way things are.

You may say, "It shouldn't be this way. I'm sowing good seed." Well, when you get your own planet, you can rearrange this whole deal, but on this planet, you're a guest. You have to take some circumstances one at a time as it comes.

# Key phrase: Discipline your disappointment.

The secret to the ambitious sower with good seed is that he continued to sow. He had to discipline his disappointment. This is a key phrase and mindset to use the rest of your life.

You must learn to discipline your disappointment because you didn't set up the setup, and some are not going to stay and that is not of your making, not your fault.

Now, of course, if you made gross errors and you ran them off, that's different—you're responsible for that. But if it's in the normal course of things, this is the way things are.

The story continues saying that the next seed sown falls on thorny ground. By this point you may be wondering, *How much of this do I have to go through?* Well, hang on. It's not the end of the story.

The seed falls on thorny ground, and now a little plant starts to grow. But as the plant grows, the thorns choke it to death, and it dies. Thorns are going to get some; that's just the way it is. And what are these thorns? The story calls them little cares, little distractions, little somethings that keep the plant from growing.

"John, we had a meeting last night. You weren't there."

John says, "Well, I can't make every meeting."

"Why not?"

He said, "Well, the screen door came off the hinges, and I just can't let my house fall apart. I got to take some time and fix things up."

And I can hear the thorns laughing, "Ha!"

He says, "And some extra trash had piled up in the garage. I can't let mountains of trash takeover. I have to keep the trash hauled out."

"Ha!"

People who let little things cheat them out of big opportunities, more often than not have regrets when they look back over their decisions.

What could you do about that? Nothing. It's just the way it is. Like winter following fall and spring following winter. The thorns are going to get some.

## GOOD SEED ON GOOD GROUND

Now, here's the good news! The sower keeps sowing the seed, keeps sharing the story, keeps inviting.

And yes, the invitation can be more powerful a year later than the first month because now it can be shared that I'm making twice as much money part-time as I'm making in my full-time job. And the law of average is still working.

Finally, the seed falls on good ground—and it always will if you keep sowing. If you share a good idea long enough, it will fall on good people.

Some of the good ground produced 30 percent, and some of the good ground produced 60 percent, and some of the good ground produced 100 percent. Why the difference in what was produced? It's just the way it is.

## ABSOLUTE TRUST

Many, many years ago, I had a unique experience that developed for me something called *absolute trust*. I can't really explain it. It's probably more of a mystery to me than it is a

# Key phrase:
# If you share a good idea long enough, it will fall on good people.

reality, but it's there. And it helped to establish my very simple theology, which goes like this.

Number one, I believe God is just, which means I'm probably in trouble. Number two, I believe God's mercy endures forever, which means I probably have an excellent chance.

It's an incredible feeling, absolute trust. It's like being financially independent. My father said, "Son, someday you have to know this incredible feeling where nobody, nor anything, has a claim on you or your assets. It's an incredible feeling, and until you get there, you really don't know what it's like. Someone can't tell you."

And I think it's true of absolute trust. It is so unique that I don't even know how to teach it. All I know is it wonderfully happened for me all those years ago, and it helps me even with my high-profile, busy, chase-around-the world to share ideas kind of life.

Absolute trust gives me an underlying serenity that is absolutely incredible. It makes the days busy but peaceful. It makes the months highly active but keeps me anchored. I think the seeds of the idea and the experience came from my parents, who laid a fantastic foundation for me when I was growing up.

I've lived an extraordinary life, and if I was to pick one thing that serves me so well in traveling the world, talking to people, being an entrepreneur, busy as can be, hopefully for another 40 years—it is this idea of absolute trust.

There's a little but mighty phrase that's helpful for everyone—God is in control. If you can finally come to that conclusion, that is the beginning of absolute trust. God's in control. Once I really believed that, I started sleeping soundly.

There are some things that should make you worry. If you're in the midst of a battle and you walk into the general's tent and he's sobbing, it's time to worry. Otherwise, knowing and trusting that God is in control can keep worry at bay.

Ultimately, trusting that God's in control and he has designed for it all to work out is fine with me. If life seems turbulent and doesn't seem to fit together at the moment, I can get through that easily by looking beyond the moment to the One who is in charge.

Faith is when you don't have any facts or anything to prove. You need faith. If everything could be proven by facts and figures, you wouldn't need faith. Faith is an extraordinary human possibility to see things that don't exist, to believe when there doesn't seem to be any factual support. So that's where trust, absolute trust and faith comes in to calm every storm.

## FINANCIAL INDEPENDENCE

Let's talk now about financial independence. First, my definition of financial independence is *the ability to live from the income of your personal resources*. This should be every person's definition who lives in a free country, especially a capitalistic country. This should be everyone's goal to someday be able to live from the income of their personal resources.

How many resources you need depends on how you want to live. If you wish to live modestly, it doesn't take many resources over a fairly brief period of time to have enough resources to live modestly. If you wish to live more lavishly, of course, you need to accumulate more resources. That's my view of financial independence—living from the income of your resources.

Now, here's what else that does. You can choose the work you do. You can choose to work or not work. You can work not because you *have* to but because you *want* to. When we talk to kids about financial independence, we say, "Do what you *have* to do as quickly as you can, so you can do what you *want* to do as long as you can."

# Key phrase:
# Economics is major.

The next key phrase is economics is major. Everybody should major in economics because it's such a vital part of your life. A paycheck is so vital because first of all, it provides for you and the family's survival. Second, it provides for the opportunity of success.

Some people feel we shouldn't spend that much time talking about money, but we really should. Someone says, "Well, money is the root of all evil." Not true. Here's what the Good Book really says, "The *love* of money is the root of all evil." I'm sure you have dispensed with the idea of falling in love with money because that serves no purpose.

Here's what's noble—what you can do with money. The projects it can support. The relief from debt it can create. Building a secure financial wall around your family. If you earn a lot, you should give a lot. Key phrase from antiquity: "If you've been given much, much is required. If you've been given great responsibility, much is required. If you've been given much wealth, much is required."

Everyone has to solve these questions about the money to go forward. Should you focus on earning money? Should you go for success? I believe you should earn as much as you possibly can in the reasonable time while balancing your life with everything else. Working for financial independence should not be done at the sacrifice of your family, friendships, not at the sacrifice of your values and integrity—balance of it all is vital. Go as far as you can, earn as much as you can, share as much as you can.

Ask yourself, "Is it possible in the United States of America to multiply your income by 10?" The answer is of course, yes.

If you multiply the current hourly minimum wage by 10, can you think of anybody who makes $500 an hour? The

Beverly Hills lawyers where I live make at least $500 an hour. Now, multiply income by 10 again. Would it be possible to multiply your income by 10 and then multiplied by 10 again? I'm trying to make you a believer. The scripture says, "To those who believe, all things are possible." Nothing is impossible. The most incredible things are possible to believers, not hopers—believers.

I lecture with Norman Schwarzkopf, the old general. Guess what he gets paid for his speech? $65,000 for one hour. $65,000, not $5,000, $65,000.

I had lunch with Colin Powell when I was on a speaking panel for one of those multi-speaker seminars. I think he got paid something like $70,000. It's a fun lunch with somebody who gets paid $75,000 per hour. Unbelievable.

Bill Gates made $68 million in one year. Some ask, "Is that legitimate to pay someone $68 million in one year?" And the answer is, of course. If the person helped the company make a billion dollars that year, could the company afford to pay him $68 million? The answer is yes. It's chicken feed.

Which brings us to the next chapter and key phrase—*everything is relative.*

# 6

# EVERYTHING
# IS RELATIVE

## TWO DIFFERENT PHILOSOPHIES

There are two philosophies when it comes to managing financial resources—one of the rich and one of the poor. First, the philosophy of most people of modest means is to spend their money and invest what's left. If they have anything left over, they might save it or invest it. That's the poor philosophy—spend your money, save what's left.

Second, the philosophy of the rich is to invest their money and spend what's left. It could be the same amount of money as the modest means of people, but it is managed with a different attitude and philosophy.

So your choice is to either spend your money and save what's left. Or invest your money and spend what's left. Certainly the better philosophy is to invest your money and spend what's left.

# Key phrase: Everything is relative.

Let's talk now about what to do with a dollar. For teenagers and kids, this is an especially important topic. This is one of the best places to start when in your mid-teens and have a job. This is a great place to start, no matter your age.

Because attitude determines so much of our lives, our financial journey begins with what we do with our first dollar. It all begins with what you do with your resources—your attitude about money.

## TWO CHALLENGES

There are two challenges of life. Number one, the challenge to *developing our full potential*. Challenge number two is the *wise use of all our resources*. That sums up life in general— the development of all our potential and the wise use of all our resources.

One of our resources is time, which we have discussed throughout the first few chapters. Now, we're going to talk about the wise resource of money. When I met Mr. Shoaff, he asked me about my financial condition, "How much money have you saved and invested over the last six years?"

"Zero."

He said, "That's not a good number."

"If I had more money, I'd have a better plan."

He said, "If you had a better plan, you would have more money."

# Key phrase:
# It's not the amount that counts, it's the plan that counts.

The next key phrase to remember is that it's not the amount that counts, it's the plan that counts. So with that in mind, let's start with something as seemingly as small as $1. What should you do with it? Never spend more than 70 cents of each dollar you earn or each dollar that comes your way, by gift or by labor.

I've developed this little plan simply for suggestion; you can revise it and do whatever you want to with it. But here's what I teach based on $1. Never spend more than 70 cents. Now we have left 10 cents and another 10 cents and another 10 cents, which is 30 cents plus the 70, which is the full dollar.

Now, what do we do with the 30 cents? Here's some of the most important information I can give you—10 cents should be given to a charity, or church, or whatever worthy projects you prefer. One of the best lessons to teach kids is how to be generous. Because we teach abundance, to provide more than you can use yourself, the "be fruitful" philosophy means to produce more than you need, so you have some to share.

Some churches teach that 10 percent is a tithe, which is fine. The key is to either give this 10 cents to an institution, a church, or whatever, and let them spread it around. Let them put it where it's needed. Most charities have firsthand knowledge of the needs of the local community or neighborhood.

If you plan to give to a charity or church, ask the leadership to show you where and/or how your money will be spent. That way you will know where the 10 percent goes if you're going to tithe, which will give you great joy realizing how you are helping others in need.

The next 10 cents is called capital. Capital is any value you set aside to be invested in an enterprise that brings value to the marketplace, hoping to make a profit. That's what capital and capitalism is.

Returning to the farmer example, seed corn is capital—the seed that he sets aside to be planted in the ground, takes care of in the summer, and plans to have a profit and harvest in the fall. The farmer sets aside his seed corn. Question, would he let his family eat it? No. This seed is not to be eaten. It's to be invested, in the ground, to take a risk, cared for in the summer, harvested and multiplied in the fall. That's how it works.

# Key phrase:
# Capital is any value you set aside to be invested in an enterprise that brings value to the marketplace, hoping to make a profit.

The same is true of a portion of your money, your capital. If you set aside part of your capital for an enterprise, you will hopefully show a profit. We can teach kids the early fundamentals of capitalism.

The basic formula of starting with one dollar I've come up with and has served me well over the years:

- Don't spend more than 70 cents (on bills, entertainment, etc.).

- Give 10 cents to church or charity.

- Invest 10 cents back into your business or in an enterprise that makes a profit; let someone else use it. This is called active capital, where you actually engage in an enterprise making a profit.

- Invest 10 cents as passive capital. For example, put money in a bank that pays interest. The bank pays you for the use of this money. Or you may invest in a stock, that pays you dividends, and also there may be an increase in the value of the stock.

If you're an adult and just now starting to use this formula, you may be in such bad shape financially that you can't do the 70, 10, 10, 10. If so, you may have to do a 97, 1, 1, 1 to pay your bills. If you haven't had a good financial plan up until now, you can still use the formula which will get you in the habit of making wise decisions.

Remember, *"It's not the amount that counts, it's the plan that counts."* If you are in poor financial shape, you can start with not spending more than 97 cents, then give 1 cent to charity, and invest 1 cent for active capital and 1 cent for passive capital.

Next, the key to increase the numbers is to lower the bills you have to pay. When you start giving more to charity and investments, you won't believe how exciting it is to watch the numbers change. Remember what Shoaff said, "For things to change, *you* have to change."

If you seriously consider your financial situation today and are committed to becoming financially independent, you can definitely get to the 70, 10, 10, 10.

Today is a good day to lay out a good financial plan for the future, what to do with your money.

To expand the formula to reflect your current situation:

Don't spend more than 70% of your income.

- Give 10% to church or charity.
- Invest 10% as active capital, buy and sell to see if you can make a profit.
- Invest 10% as passive capital. Let somebody else use your money and pay you interest, dividends, stock increase, whatever.

A lady in Mexico told me, "I heard your plan ten years ago. I followed it. I'm now a millionaire. I own two different properties because you also said, 'Don't buy the second car until you've bought the second house. It's not cars that make you rich. It's real estate that makes you rich.' I'm now about to buy the third house, so I'm now giving myself the luxury of buying the third car."

Simple little ideas that make a huge difference.

Then she said, "I followed the 70, 10, 10, and 10. Taught it to other people. They're following it and getting great results too."

One thing I didn't know when I was growing up and found out at age 25—I could work both on my living and my fortune at the same time *if* I had a good plan. I give you that advice as well. Don't just work on your living, work on your fortune. Work on becoming financially independent.

Financial independence is the ability to live from the income of your personally invested resources. And the day you can do that is a great day indeed. It's exciting when you can work for joy and not for necessity. And strangely enough, you probably work a lot harder for joy than you do for necessity.

## EARNING A LIVING OR MAKING A FORTUNE

I have a unique friend who started an enterprise, and by the time he had it up and running about three years later, he didn't have to work anymore the rest of his life. Now, he's financially independent. He created such a vast fortune that for the next 20 years of his life he was working for joy, not for necessity. I encourage you to get to that position as quickly as you can.

Work both on your living and your fortune. The reason for earning a living is to make a fortune, not necessarily from your living but from what you earn because you invested wisely.

A lady the other day said, "Mr. Rohn, I'm in real estate."

"Wonderful. How many properties do you own?"

She said, "No, no, I *sell* real estate."

"Well, let me ask you one more time, how many properties do you own?"

To get my meaning across I said, "The reason for selling real estate is to earn the money to buy real estate. If you *sell* real estate, you make a living. If you *buy* real estate, you make a fortune."

She said, "Okay, I got the message. Thank you."

So don't buy the second car until you've bought the second home.

# Key phrase: Make a fortune from wise investment earnings.

## BUILDING WEALTH

The wise use of financial resources is simple, straightforward, and easy to implement, and best of all, it works. Yet most find it hard to believe that building wealth can be so simple. We think, *Should I invest conservatively or aggressively? What types of investments should I select? Should I invest when I have credit cards to pay off?*

The whole world of financial options seems unbearably complex, but I want you to resist this complexity by just picking a plan that feels right to you and most importantly—get started today.

I say, figure out what you think is best for you and try that.

Part of it is a matter of age. The older you are, the more conservative investments. Younger people tend to make bolder investments that could pay big dividends if it cashed in well. But I believe a mixture of investments with good growth prospects is best. You have to decide your own aversion to risk, whether or not you can really tolerate it.

What constitutes good money management? Consider that you can pay off your home in 15 years instead of 30 by adding just one more payment each year. A simple plan that can save you more than the price of the house! Some people really don't care about paying off the mortgage as long as their monthly payments are low. That's one philosophy, but it's not a good one.

And if you're paying 14-16 percent interest on credit cards, if you pay off those and pay off your home in 15 years instead of 30, of course, now you can buy a home, another home, get a 15-year mortgage.

Why not save? Why not be prudent? Why not be careful? It's good practice, even if you're rich. It's wise to be as prudent as you can be, not to be stingy, not to try to cheat somebody, but to do wise things with your resources.

## SECOND BIG CHALLENGE

The two big challenges in life's adventure are: 1) the full development of all of your potential, and 2) the wise use of all your resources, including your money and your time, which are two of the major resources. It is important to your success as to how you use your time and how to use your money.

For instance, I instruct adults and students alike that it's important not to have a savings account. It's important to have an investment account, just a change in terminology but a big change in philosophy. It's the same money, but the outcome is different depending where you put it. An investment account will increase your money faster than a savings account.

Sometimes, you have to ask for some professional help. Go to a credible, knowledgeable source and say, "Look, here's how deep in debt I'm in. What can I do?" Ask for good alternate plans as well. Maybe the family can't quite tolerate a severe program for the immediate future. Maybe there's one that will take a little longer. But start sooner than later—there's nothing more exhilarating, really, in terms of self-worth and self-esteem than just getting started. Just thinking *at least I'm not in reverse anymore* will keep you smiling day after day.

It's been said that "If you're in a hole, stop digging." At least stop where you are, and see if you can now build a ladder, the best one you can design at the moment, with some help. If a matter of finances and you're overwhelmed with credit card debt, I recommend you find somebody who has good strategies for getting out of debt.

There are some programs that will hold off the collection people. If convinced you have a plan, rather than push you into bankruptcy, there are organizations that will help you rearrange your finances so you can start digging your way out. It's surprising once you start making changes how excited you will be. The numbers don't have to be huge as long as you're making progress.

Do you have to be an entrepreneur, like I was, to become wealthy? Ultimately, it's your attitude and philosophy that have far more to do with how wealthy you'll become than your profession.

You can turn part of your present income, wisely use the resources from that income to make a profit, even if you let other people use the money and pay you interest in dividends. If at least you do that, whether you buy and sell or not, you can begin to make your fortune.

## WHY NOT?

If you have worked on a job for 20-30 years, why not buy a piece of property and sell it for more than you paid for it? Why not you buy a home? Sell it for more than you paid for it? Why not you buy a piece of property that needs repair? Find somebody to repair it and sell it for more than you paid for it. Why not you do that over the next 40 years, as well as work on the job and punch the clock and do your duty and retire as a faithful employee?

Why not work both on your fortune and your living? Why not? If the least you did was take part of what you've earned as a living, and let someone else use it and pay you for the use. If you did that over 40 years, you would easily be financially independent, not from your job, but from your investments.

Claude Olney, put together a program and called it "Where There's a Will, There's an A." It became a highly successful infomercial and several books. He attended my seminars years before he put that program together and said, "I've got an idea. What do you think?"

I said, "It's a winner."

Sure enough, it made him millions. He made money on every car he bought because of the incredible way he took care of it, and the way he made it shine and gleam so that when he got ready to sell, it was worth more than when he bought it. That was one of his projects. "I'm going to make money on every car I buy."

Your fortune depends on your attitude and your philosophy, and the answer is, "Why not?"

Amazing. Two different people with two different attitudes. One lets it all go because it doesn't seem to make a difference. Another one says, "I make money on whatever I touch. Whatever I touch gets better. It doesn't get dirty. It gets better."

A guy who owned several apartments said to me one day, "Most everybody leaves the apartment that they rent worse than they found it."

"Really? You've got to be kidding."

He said, "No, some leave it trashed."

How dreadful. On the other hand, imagine if everyone had the attitude or the mindset, "Wherever I am, I'm going to leave it better than I found it." Not just what it does for the world because it's a better place if you do that, but what it does for your own psyche. "Whatever I touch gets cleaner and it gets better, and it gets painted, and it gets restored. Even if I walk away."

You may say, "Well, somebody else is going to enjoy it all." So be it. That's not the key. The key is, my philosophy is that I will leave everything better than I found it.

# THREE MORE KEYS REGARDING FINANCIAL INDEPENDENCE

## 1. KEEP STRICT ACCOUNTS.

Another key on financial independence is to keep strict accounts. Part of it is just for habit, and the other part is for self-esteem, and the other part is for future benefit. Keep strict accounts about what you are doing with your money, where it's being spent, where it's being invested—keep track of all your financial resources. Keeping an accurate and timely account of your money is a good habit to have. It's like taking out the trash and arriving on time for appointments. It becomes the person you are. Keep good accounts.

## 2. PAY YOUR TAXES.

I finally became a happy taxpayer. Here's what paying taxes does—it feeds the goose that lays the golden eggs called American opportunity. You say, "Well, the goose eats too much." Probably true, but make the note: better a fat goose than no goose.

## 3. EVERYONE SHOULD PAY TAXES.

Here's the next key—everybody should pay. My personal philosophy is everyone should pay federal taxes, as well as state taxes, and whatever else. It is not wise for the government to let one-third of American citizens off the federal tax rolls. Why? Because not paying taxes robs people of their dignity—of being part of the process. All citizens should pay their fair share of taxes—no matter where they land on the income scale.

I've had in mind for a long time writing a book titled *Of Course Kids Should Pay Taxes*. Why? Because when a kid in California walks into 7-Eleven and buys something that costs a dollar, the proprietor asks the kid for eight more pennies.

The kid says, "What's the eight pennies for?"

He says, "That's for taxes."

The kid says, "But I'm only eight years old."

And the proprietor says, "Congratulations, you're my youngest taxpayer. Give me the money."

Should kids pay taxes? Yes. If you want to ride your bicycle on the sidewalk instead of in the mud, you have to cough up the eight pennies. Taxes pay for sidewalks.

What if you're poor? Do you pay the eight pennies? Yes. What if you're rich? Yes. Meaning everybody should pay state and local taxes. The same should apply to federal taxes. I don't care if it's $10 a year or $100 a year or $1000 a year. Regardless of your income, you have to say, "No matter how poor I am at the moment, I will make my contribution to the community (the state, the country)." That's the key to keeping society running as smoothly as possible. Everybody should pay taxes.

Taxes pay for our military who keep our country safe and secure. We have to pay some young volunteer who risks his life on night landings on an aircraft carrier. If you want that kind of security in the world, you have to pay. Of course, we may disagree sometimes with government policy and all the rest, but that doesn't negate our responsibility to pay.

The following is one of the best stories ever written regarding giving. According to the record, one day Jesus and His disciples were at the synagogue. And on this occasion they had an interesting project, to stand outside the synagogue as people entered and watch them put money in the synagogue's treasury. They noticed that some people gave large amounts, some came by with modest amounts, and others gave small amounts.

Then along comes a little lady who puts two pennies in the treasury.

And Jesus said to His disciples, "Look at that."

They said, "Two pennies. What's two pennies?"

He says, "No, you don't understand. She gave more than everybody else."

They said, "Two pennies is more than everybody else's offerings?"

He said, "Yes because I'm positive her two pennies represented most of what she had. So since she gave most of what she had, she gave the most."

When the little lady put two pennies in the treasury and walked away, *here's what did not occur*. Jesus did *not* run after her and say, "Hold it. Hold it, little lady. My disciples and I have decided that because you're so pitiful and you're so poor, we have decided to take the two pennies out of the treasury and give them back to you."

That did not occur. If it would have occurred, the lady would have been insulted. She may have said, "Hey, it was only two pennies, but it was most of what I had. Would you rob me of the joy of giving my two pennies?"

Jesus left her two pennies in the treasury, even though she was poor. What does that mean? Everybody should pay, should contribute to the greater good of all, even if it's only two pennies.

# 7

# TIME PROTECTION AND MANAGEMENT

To maintain the momentum generated by your initial excitement about turning any area of your life around, you need to learn to master the use of your time. This involves not only the skill of time management, but the skill of time protection in our modern world of increasing distractions, unwanted interruptions, and noise—we must be able to protect our time and preserve it for our highest priorities.

Time is precious. Life is not just the passing of time. Life is a collection of experiences, their frequency, and their intensity. Life is not just watching the clock tick away. When my friend Mark died at age 44, someone said, "That's too young to die." But what if he lived four lifetimes in one? It might not be too young. Whatever the span of our lives turns out to be, I believe we should want to fill it up with experiences and the intensity of those experiences.

# APPROACHES TO TIME PROTECTION AND MANAGEMENT

Now let's talk about time and the approaches to the management and protection of time.

## 1. DON'T WORK HARDER, WORK SMARTER.

Years ago, I worked longer and harder, but there's a limit to that approach. I almost lost my health in the first year. I went so crazy about personal development and achievement that I went bonkers. I told you I was skinny. By the end of that first year, I was a walking shadow. Then it suddenly occurred to me, *What if I get rich but am too ill to enjoy it?* That realization was a shocker. Working longer and harder for some might be appropriate—but in the long run, you can only work so hard for so long.

So the key is not to work harder, but smarter. When you've worked as hard as you can, doing the best you can in terms of physical output in a reasonable time, and you're not getting the desired results, you must become more skillful. This is the ultimate solution in the management of time—you simply become more skillful.

When I first entered into sales, my colleagues were people who could make 8 or 9 out of 10 sales. When I first started, I could only get 1 sale out of 10. So, I worked around the clock to make up in numbers what I lacked in skill. That's a good strategy in sales. When you're new, you make up in numbers what you lack in skill.

When you become more skillful, you don't have to work as hard. But at first, if you want to compete or if you want to really get good, you have to put in the hard work and time. When you get more from yourself and develop more of yourself, time management becomes an easier task.

## 2. EITHER YOU RUN THE PROJECT OR IT RUNS YOU—TAKE CHARGE.

I found out that when I started something, at first I was in charge. Then, a year later, I realized it was in charge. I was in charge of the companies I started, I was in control. A couple of years later, I'm out of control, on the run, and dizzy trying to get all the work all done. The key is to take charge.

It's easy to start something—and it's easy to lose control of it as it continues to grow. From personal experience, the enterprise I started expanded to 13 offices encompassing a large entourage. It was short nights and long days and a never-ceasing demand for my time and activity. At that time in my life, it was fine and created a lot of good results and laid some good foundation for a lot of future careers. In fact I have a pretty long list of people who were inspired by it and educated by it and participated in the program. But then I changed the format to accommodate my own life personally, which has paid off for me.

I still have a heavy workload, but most everything is done for me. For instance, I still farm in Idaho, but now I'm known as a "gentleman farmer." A gentleman farmer gives orders and other people do the work. It's different from being a farmer doing the work yourself. I was raised in the farm country where I still have my farm. And now I have the luxury of participants who look after my agriculture, my home building; and my daughter looks after all of my accounts, residences, and my real estate. I also have good business partners. That's extra luxury where you can do your specialty and other people are working to make it valuable.

One of my books is titled *Take Charge of Your Life*. Similarly, I could write books titled: Take charge of your time, take charge of your resources, and take charge of your health. But it all comes down to you. You're the one responsible for your life.

It's not a requirement of society that you remain healthy and take care of your family—it's up to you to make those requirements of yourself. Society doesn't require that you build a financial safety wall around your family. It's a requirement you impose on yourself to build a financial wall around your family so nothing can invade their security. Impose on yourself self-development of taking charge of your life and your health and your future and your responsibilities, and all the rest.

## 3. REASONABLE TIME IS ENOUGH TIME TO ACHIEVE ALL OF YOUR GOALS.

I had to learn that reasonable time is enough time, which led me to realize that *it's not the hours you put in, it's what you put in the hours*. If you start depositing greater ideas into the hours you have, you won't believe the productivity that will flow! The ideas will start to flow when you deposit those ideas in the hours you have—and productivity multiplies by 2, 5, 10, who knows!

## 4. WRITE A SET OF GOALS AND PRIORITIES.

Before you write, answer these questions: What are my goals? What is important this week? What's important this month?

After you write your goals and priorities, review often, go over your goals to make sure your list is working for you—it inspires you. Someone may ask you along the way, "Why are you up so early?" Say, "If you were headed where I'm headed, you'd be up early too. If you were going to meet who I'm going to meet, you'd be up early. If it was going to stack up for you like it's stacking up for me, you'd be getting up early too!"

## 5. LEARN TO STUDY THE MAJORS AND MINORS.

Determine what is critical and what is routine. For example, before you pick up the phone to make a call, think, *Is this going to be a major conversation or a minor conversation? If it's minor, a few pleasantries and I'm done. If major, maybe I should make a few notes beforehand.*

Important conversations may require writing an agenda before you make the call. It's too easy to just talk out of your head, and doing so may lead to ending a conversation like this: "Umm, let's see. There was something else I wanted to bring up, hmm...I can't think of it right now. I'll call you back." That type of uncertainty will make you seem a little incompetent. Write an agenda before you make an important call—and take notes during the call to ensure you have covered all the vital points. This simple step will save you from having head-aches later.

For example, when you follow up with the salesman in a couple of weeks, the conversation may go like this: "Hi, John, remember those four things we went over in our last phone call?"

"No, we didn't talk about that," he responds.

**125**

Then you pull out the agenda you had for the call—and there are your points and your notes, which you recite to John.

"Oh yes, seems like I do remember," he says.

Salespeople especially can talk people out of what's only in their heads. And if you don't have a little proof, it's gone. Make an agenda before you make a call.

# Key phrase: Don't major in the minor.

*Key: Don't major in minor things.* If you take up major time to do minor things, you'll be constantly behind the curve. In sales training, *minor time is:* thinking about prospects; making lists of prospects; keeping books on prospects; going to see the prospect; evaluating the prospect after you've met. That's all minor time.

*Major time is being in the presence of the prospect.* If you're in sales and you look back at a week's activities and see that you're spending 90 percent of your time on minor stuff, you know you have to make a change. Ask yourself, *How many hours of my sales week am I in the presence of a prospect—major time?* That is the time that really counts—being in the presence of the prospect.

## 6. DON'T MISTAKE MOVEMENT FOR ACHIEVEMENT.

This is another essential in time protection and management. It's easy to get faked out by being busy. Guy comes home at night, all exhausted, falls in the chair, and says, "Oh, I've been going, going, going." Here's the big question. Doing what? Some people are going, going, going, and all they're doing are figure eights. They're not making much progress. So don't mistake movement for achievement.

## 7. DON'T MISTAKE COURTESY FOR CONSENT.

This is also in sales training. If somebody's pleasant and they nod, you may think, *Oh, they're going to buy.* No, they may just be courteous. You can't mistake courtesy for consent.

## 8. CONCENTRATE.

I learned the art of concentration years ago when I was in the shower trying to compose a letter. It turned out to be a strange letter. As a result, I learned to save the work until I got to the office. Save the work until you get to the work. Don't try to get to the office on the way to work; on the way to work, enjoy the way. In the shower, enjoy the shower. Then go to work when you get to work. I found this lesson to be very helpful—concentrate.

## 9. LEARN TO SAY "NO."

Learning to say no is crucial in managing your time. In such a social society we have now, it's so easy to try to be a nice person saying yes, yes, yes to everything. You will quickly find yourself overloaded with the minor with no time for the major. Choose where you spend your time but not saying yes too quickly. When invited to a minor, respond with a comment such as, "Thank you very much, but I don't think I can fit it in my already-made commitments. But if anything changes, I'll call you." My friend Ron Reynolds says, "Don't let your mouth overload your back." It's a good one.

## 10. DON'T PLAY AT WORK, DON'T WORK AT PLAY.

When you work, work; when you play, play—don't mix the two. Work is serious. You don't want the reputation of being the office joker. It's not a good reputation to have. Yes, there is time for some pleasant stories. Yes, there's time for a little humor. Yes, best if it's a happy office, of course. But you have to be serious about work because you're parting with a piece of your life for the work you do. Your work costs you a piece of your life. It's called serious business—not grim, not unhappy, but serious. Don't play at work. Treat work with all due conservative passion because it's leading you to your future.

## 11. RECOGNIZE YOUR WEAKNESSES.

Take time to analyze any weaknesses you have and if they are wasting your time. A personal example, I used to keep promising myself to work on the financial accounting books. But then I realized that chore wasn't one I was good at and took too much of my time away from the major. Finally I gave up and hired an accountant to keep the books and it only cost me about $60 back then. Sort out your weaknesses and make changes if necessary.

## 12. BEWARE OF DISTRACTIONS.

Beware of how much time you spend on the telephone and all other systems of communication, at work and at home. Let all communication systems serve you, but don't let them intrude.

When it comes time to have dinner with your family, shut off all systems except perhaps ones that can take messages silently. Don't let the phone ring. Don't let anybody intrude on the family time, which is important. No one should come through the front door, back door, telephone, or any other device. Neither John nor the President of the United States should disturb the time you spend with family. If you develop that kind of a reputation, father, mother, when we have dinner, when we're visiting and have this time with our family, nothing intrudes. Don't allow any clever little devices to intrude, distract, or disturb. You have to have a place and time that's sacrosanct. It's valuable. Don't let anything in for that period of time. And likewise, be respectful of other people's family meal time.

I asked a guy many years ago, "What did your television cost?" I knew he was a great television watcher.

He said, "Four hundred dollars."

"That's not true."

He said, "Yes it is, I paid four hundred dollars for this television set."

"Well, let me tell you what I think it's costing you because I know what kind of talent and skills you have. I think it's costing you about $40,000 a year not to own it but to *watch* it."

It's not *owning* a television set that's expensive; it's *watching* it that's expensive. What else could you do at that time; one, you've got plenty of money in terms of lifestyle, but if you haven't got plenty of money, what if you took the television time and properly employed it by learning a couple of extra skills? No telling what would happen to your income.

I mentioned all this to the guy and he got so inspired and convicted with my little talk that he had his brother-in-law come over in his pickup and haul away his television set.

He said, "I have a new philosophy. I'm going to take my TV time and turn it into fortune."

All it takes is an idea, and it doesn't have to be that radical, but he wanted it to make a statement. Later he had another television, but by then, he learned to shut it off and use time wisely. At the moment, he wanted to prove to himself that he was ready to do something radical. He said, "Jim Rohn is right. This television is costing me a fortune. Owning it is cheap. Watching it is expensive."

Television is useful but use it wisely. Just like food, use it wisely. In leadership, we teach to eat enough food to be healthy and gather strength—and no more. You have to learn the "no more." Make that your philosophy. How much rest? Enough to be healthy and gather strength—and no more. Why would you spend any more than just enough to gather strength and be healthy on both food and rest?

# Key phrase: Learn to ration your time.

If you overindulge in food and rest, they become detriments, not life support. I think that's a great way to look at life; let essentials serve but not intrude. If you let television serve, fine, but if you let it intrude—that's not fine. It's said that the average person watches television five hours a day. I think that's probably too much. It's not that the television isn't good, it is good, but people devote too much time watching it when there are many other more productive ways to spend time. Let it serve, not intrude is a good philosophy. The same is true for computers and the time spent online.

When you have a healthy philosophy and attitude that turns your life around, it sets the tone for what you do, don't do, correct, rearrange, and fits the lifestyle you desire. If you find yourself addicted, unable to "let go," you know you have a problem. It doesn't matter whether it's alcohol or drugs or a computer, it's possible to be online and off track. Protecting your time also prevents issues that can quickly get out of control.

## 13. TAKE A STEP DOWN, OR BACK.

Step down to something easier. The guy is in sales and says, "I want to own the company." Eventually he owns the company. But now he has no time to play golf. Now he says, "When I was in sales, I was making big money and playing golf three days a week. Heck, now that I'm an owner, my life is never my own."

If you're too pressed and life isn't as excellent as you expected, you might consider stepping down or stepping back into a lifestyle with less time pressure.

A perfect example: A little girl says to her mother, "Daddy comes home with his briefcase and pats me on the head and says, 'Hello,' then he disappears and works on his papers. Why doesn't Daddy play with me?"

Her mother says, "Your daddy loves you very much, but he's so busy at work, he can't get it all done. He has to bring it home. He loves you, but that's why he can't play with you."

And the little girl says, "Why don't they just put him in a slower group?"

If you don't have time for your kids, you might consider joining a slower group. Remember when I said some things I went for cost me too much? I urge you to reconsider.

## 14. THINK!

What absorbs your attention? Be mindful of where your focus is. If all of your thoughtful time is used for busy time rather than creative time, then the encroachment on your creative time is too heavy. We need time to think. Napoleon Hill's best-selling book title is *Think and Grow Rich*. Nowadays they say,

"Get online and find all the answers." Hill says, in essence, "No. Think. Think and grow. Think and grow rich. Think of better ways to do things. Think of better times. Think of better ways to be creative, not just busy."

## 15. LEARN TO ASK QUESTIONS UPFRONT.

This is a great time management saver. Asking questions upfront helps you get to the issue or problem quickly. Don't just launch into some discourse and waste 30 minutes or an hour when you could have been solving the problem. Don't talk around the issue and don't allow the other person to evade the prime issue. Ask questions upfront.

## 16. LEARN TO THINK ON PAPER.

One way to solve problems is to take it out of your head and put it on paper. Another way is to set goals and write each one on paper, along with other details. Another good way to think on paper is to create a project book. Write in a booklet or tablet the name of each person you're working with and the name of the project. Then write a brief, continual summary of how it's going between you and the person and between you and the project. This has been very useful to me. Each time you get together, you can review your notes and know better what to talk about.

When the president gets ready to travel and he's going to meet important people, he's given briefing books. For example, I can imagine the conversation going something like this, "The last time you were with Khrushchev," Kennedy is informed, "here's what he said, and here's what you said." Kennedy says, "Oh, that's valuable. I need to remember that."

To make a good impression, to keep yourself current, and to bring order to a project or meeting, take the time to keep project books.

## 16A. KEEP TRACK OF ALL YOUR APPOINTMENTS.

Part of thinking on paper includes an appointment calendar. There are many appointment calendars available today. Keeping track of all that's going on in your life—professional and personal—is vital. Mine is filled with details including when and where the plane departs, what time the seminar begins, where the conference is being held, and all the rest of what is scheduled. Also keep track of when your bills are due—house and car insurance, etc. Take these dates out of your head and put them in your calendar.

The last thinking on paper key is to keep a journal. I'm known around the world for keeping a journal—have been now for about 40 years. My journal is not necessarily a diary. It might be part diary. I may be flying over Ireland and I write down a few little things that impressed me such as: *Today I met _____. Wow, what an extraordinary event. Today I conducted a seminar in Rome. A thousand people stood up and sang for me.* I have a little bit of a diary in there but primarily my journal is for collecting good ideas.

A journal is to collect good ideas on your health, your business, your future, and good ideas for time management. I used to take notes on pieces of paper and torn off corners and backs of old envelopes and restaurant place mats, and then I threw all this stuff in a drawer. This method did not serve me well. I finally bought a journal and carry it almost everywhere. If you're caught without your journal, take notes and then put those notes in your journal when you get home or back to the office. My journals now make up a significant part of my library. My journals are all reserved privately for my children and my grandchildren. Can you imagine what I've collected over the years? It's unbelievable.

## LEAVE-BEHIND TREASURES

There are three treasures to leave behind: your photographs, library, and journals.

Number one, your pictures. Don't leave any event unrecorded. It takes only a fraction of a second to say, "Here's who I was with." When I travel the world, we take pictures of the people and places and gifts. They are part of the treasures I keep on the farm. It's true that a picture is worth a thousand words to describe the scene, the emotion, and what happened. A photo brings back memories; *This was an extraordinary day for me when I met these people at a seminar ten years ago.* Wow, the drama comes back.

What would it be like if you had thousands of photographs of the past, of your history, your mother, your father, grandparents? You can leave those traces of yourself for your children and your children's children. Leave all your photographs as a record.

Number two, your library. Leave behind for others the books that changed your life, the books that changed your health, the books that rescued you from oblivion, the books that you passed on to other people. They were so exciting for you. The books that made you financially independent, the books that developed your leadership, books that gave you wisdom to ponder when things were tough. The books that got you through the winter, the books that helped you to plant in the spring and harvest in the fall. What a treasure to leave behind. If you leave behind your library, for sure, your books will be more valuable than your furniture.

The third treasure to leave behind is your journals, the notes you took that helped you to live life as you lived it. Long after you're gone, these will be treasures that your children, grandchildren, and great-grandchildren will find so fascinating. They may even use what they read to help guide their own life into their own future.

Wow.

# 8

# FAMILY AND FRIENDSHIP

Ironically, the achievement of great career success, and often the desire of someone who wishes to turn their life around can itself cause other areas of their life to be neglected. The area that is most often neglected when such success occurs is our close relationships with family and friends. We don't spend the time with our spouses that we used to. And sometimes we have a short fuse with our children at the end of a difficult day. We think back and realize that it's been years since we talked to the best man or maid of honor from our wedding. Yet, statistics show that relationships account for more than 80 percent of our happiness in life.

Are you in need of a change in this area of your life—or just a little reminding about what is truly important—where true wealth really lies.

## PAY ATTENTION TO DETAILS

We have to pay attention to the details when it comes to relationships. Don't let too much time pass without staying in touch with family and friends. If you think of the 20 most important people in your life, how long has it been since you sat down with or called or wrote to each of those 20 people? I encourage you to write a list of those 20 important people and then make a serious effort to contact them. I have a good feeling if you call and say, "Wow, it's been too long. Let's have lunch. Let's get together," that you will receive a warm and positive response.

Some may live in your community so it's easier to stay in touch, but some friends are not close by. Staying in touch is an important part of developing good relationships. Take care of what matters. If nobody calls you on your birthday, that may not matter to you. But for some of your family or friends, it does matter. Make sure those kinds of gestures are done. It's easy, especially in our fast-paced society, to be so busy doing that you don't think you can find time to reach out with the small but kind effort. It may be easy to let things slide, but we will most probably have regrets later if we don't stay in touch more often, especially if someone older passes. Then we quickly say, "Wow, I should have made more phone calls and stayed in touch."

A good relationship is like taking care of a garden. You can't let it go too long without tending to what makes it flourish and keeping it well-nourished, which is true of all of our valuables. We must protect them like a father and nourish them like a mother. To make sure they give us full value and then be of full value to them. Not that you have to be around all the time but to be available.

There's an ancient phrase that says if you try to save your life, you will lose it; but if you will lose your life, meaning if you will invest your life, that's the best way to save it and to multiply it many times over. Here's the phrase, investing life into life has the potential of creating miracles.

Investing life into life creates a new baby, but investing life into life with ideas, information, association, and influence can create an enterprise, a corporation, a business, a movement, and something that benefits many more people than just those few who might have invested in each other's lives. That should be one of your goals—to be valuable enough to invest in somebody else's life, starting first if you're married with your children and then invest in each other.

Marriage and friendships provide opportunities to invest in each other—personally and professionally.

Bill Bailey and I had been involved in enterprises, and one enterprise became very successful and affected many other people's lives. Over the years, we continued to invest in each

# Key phrase:
# Investing life into life has the potential to create miracles.

other. When I came up with a great idea. I called him. When he read a good book, he'd tell me, "This is a masterpiece. You've got to read it." We invested in each other while walking the farm country of Kentucky, the beaches of California, wherever possible. He had a habit of grabbing my arm when we were walking and talking. We appreciated the chances to contribute to each other, to share with each other. Just like I am sharing what I've learned with you, my reader. The contribution of sharing with each other, being influential, providing leadership, making a positive difference in someone's life can be of such a magnitude that there is no telling how far it may go from the time it starts.

## INNER CIRCLE INFLUENCE

Friendship is one of the most valuable possessions in the world. Good friends, relationships. What really matters when we all get right down to it is that inner circle of ours—those with whom we should spend as much quality time as possible—because that's where a lot of the drive and ambition to do well comes from, for them and for us. Making dreams come true for your inner circle furnishes the fuel for your own high ambition. Not to be ambitious just for the name or for the fame or for the money or for the useful things you can do like generosity for the future, but to do as much as you can to nourish your association and communication with those who matter most, your inner circle.

Conversation is an art, whether with a child, spouse, or friends. Years ago, people wrote letters that that were sent or received only once in a while. Back then people took thoughtful care about putting into words how they really felt, what was happening in their lives and community. Now with the ease of phoning anywhere anytime, it's easy to be too casual in conversations. Too easy to lose the meaning of an experience when lost in mundane, ordinary conversations that are the norm. Rather, take time to say something unique and supportive about the other person, how you care, and how you feel.

When Judy, my wife, and I parted ways, I wrote a little note: "Dear Judy, as often as the night comes, so does my sadness. As constant as the day arrives, so is my love for you. I wish the best for you. I understand that dilemma. My life is here where you touched me. If ever you should call, I will be there to be touched again." I took a little time to thoughtfully see if I could say in a very few words what was happening to me at the time. It is easy to be careless with language and not say what you mean to get a point across.

There is no greater opportunity to practice the art of conversation and your ability to invest life into life than parenthood, or in my case, grand-parenthood. It is said that parenting is the toughest job you'll ever love—it is an investment that produces a wealth of spirit out of all proportion to your investment.

## BECOMING A WORLD-CLASS PARENT AND GRANDPARENT

Each new occasion is a chance to be this one expression called "born again" or "reborn." When a baby arrives for the first time, we have a new father for the first time as well. The baby is starting a life to live and the new father is also starting a new life to live. The same is true for a first-time baby and a first-time mother. Each has the opportunity to live a brand-new life, a different life experience than ever before. Shouldn't parents study and practice and learn and listen in an effort to find ways to become a Class A mother or father?

About 16 years ago, I became a grandfather, and I have practiced diligently over those years to be a five-star grandfather to my two grandchildren, Nathaniel and Natalie. I must say they're exceptional, highly talented. I just published a book of my granddaughter's poems that she wrote when she was 12, which includes the art illustrations by her brother Nathaniel. *I Love What I See* is the title, by Natalie Pangrazio. Now she's 15 and she's written a collection of 10 stories for children, and her brother, Nathaniel, is an accomplished classical pianist who writes music and sends off his creations for competition. These are talented kids, artists and writers and musicians at such a young age.

Along the way, all I've done is pay attention to them. Listen to them. Help them as they tried their wings at this and that. One of the poems Natalie wrote when she was 12 is titled "Metaphors of Flowers":

> From those whose imaginations love to take flight,
>
> they will use even a flower to determine wrong from right.
>
> Irises like wisdom, the deep color like the depth of knowledge and the yellow like the bright ideas one receives, the knowledge spreads upwards as do the iris's leaves.
>
> A lily, a simplicity like the whiteness of its flower,

but in simplicity, there is beauty like the yellow stamens tower.

Truth is like a dandelion, which is bold and has not sinned.

Truth is spread far and wide like dandelion seeds upon the wind.

They soon find a place to rest and grow in some-one's heart

and the cycle begins again just as it did start.

A daisy is like happiness and spreads its face to the sun.

It loves everything around it and in everything finds fun.

Hate is like a thistle, which is awful and sharp to the touch.

It combines envy, anger, and most of all disgust.

Finally, best of all, love represents a rose.

Love is sweet to your heart as a rose is to your nose.

Love combines trust, hope, faith and integrity.

There are good paths and bad paths and no matter which one you chose,

love is just as sweet as the loveliest rose.

My 12-year-old granddaughter wrote that. Incredible.

## BE AVAILABLE AND CAPABLE

Do everything you can think of to dazzle your children and grandchildren, to have them think you're the greatest and the best ever—it's pure joy. But you have to pay attention. There is some work involved, of course, in making a good relationship like that work, but the payoff is incredible for the small price to pay. You can be part of the day that turns their life around!

One of my dear friends asked me, "I have teenagers now. What more can I do at this age to influence their life?"

I said, "Maybe not that much, but here's two good words to consider now that they're teenagers. The key is to be *available* and *capable*. Capable of good answers when they need them, capable of counsel when they need it, available when they need to make a call. Trying to daily influence somebody's life after they've become ,especially, teenagers is a tough job."

Nevertheless, if you make an effort to be available and capable, your teens will appreciate it. Also, be well-read and have a good command of language so you can translate your own feelings and experiences into useful conversations when the need arises. Have something valuable and wise to say, however short or long it may be.

It's like fishing. You can't jerk too hard or you lose them. You can't leave too much slack and let them off the line. Then they're gone. It's called pull, pull, pull. Easy, easy pull, pull, easy, easy to learn how to fish, to catch fish. It's kind of the same with communication with children. Strong enough but not too strong. It can't be weak or the point doesn't get across. It has to be strong, strong without being rude, I say in one sense.

It's more like just being a presence, physically and also in communication. Well-chosen words mixed with measured emotion will gain their attention. Not too much, not too little. When the actor gives a performance, if the script is well-written, that's part of the structure. The rest is delivery. Part of it is style, but part of it is enough emotion for the point, not too much, and I think parents have to do the same.

Sometimes, kids have a valid objection to saying, "It's not that big a deal." In the parents' mind, it's a monster deal when it really isn't. If you always make everything into a big deal when it isn't, kids get a bit misled by that. The key is to save up that emotional content of making something a big deal if it's a big deal—and be a little more rational and emotionally contained when it isn't such a big deal. More thoughtful than volume, more caring than loud.

It's an art. It's a bit tricky dealing with kids. Right? You have to tell them what you love and what you hate. "I love you, but I hate what's happening." They need to know both. How do you put both strong feelings in the same sentence? Find a way. We have to deal with both. What's right, what's wrong, what's better? What's okay? What would be better? We all struggle with the language.

Words are clumsy sometimes when you try to express what's going on in your head, let alone your heart—it's not an easy challenge, but it's how you build empires, strong family relationships. It's how you create great societies. It's how you share the intricacies of philosophy that can change somebody's life. Whether you have a unique, rational conversation with a child, with a son or a daughter, grandson or granddaughter, or whether it's the president having a rational conversation with the country, make it unique to your audience of one or many to get the point across.

## I'M HAPPY, YOU'RE HAPPY

If you're married and have children, I have some great advice for you, the best I can give you. If the parents are okay, the kids are okay. Chances are high that if the parents are happy, the kids are happy. Your own self-development is the best contribution you can give to your children, not self-sacrifice. Self-sacrifice usually earns contempt. Self-development and self-investment earn respect.

I used to use the old phrase, "I'll take care of you, you take care of me." But I realized how short-ended that statement was. So I changed it with the help of Bob Cummings, the movie star, to: I'll take care of me for you, if you'll take care of you for me. The best contribution I can make to you if you're my child or even friend, is my personal development. What if I become 10 times wiser, 10 times stronger, 10 times better, 10 times more unique? Think of what that will do for your children, grandchildren, and friendships. If parents multiply their own personal values by two, three, five, or by 10, what would that do for their children? Everything! Wow.

If you as a parent are happy, I'm telling you, your kids will be happy. If parents engage in a unique lifestyle of mutual respect and responsibility, children will feel secure and loved. A prime example: A flight attendant tells the passengers that if the plane experiences an emergency, oxygen masks will drop down. Then they are told, "Make sure you take care of your children first." NO. The passengers are actually told to *take care of yourself first.* That's key—take care of yourself first, then assist your children. (That would be a good title of a book for parents, wouldn't it? *Put your mask on first.*)

# Key phrase:
# Take care of yourself first.

Likewise, the best contribution to your company is your self-development. The best contribution to your husband or your wife is your personal development to become all you can, become as wise as you can and as kind as you can and as unique as you can. That's the best contribution, self-investment is key.

## DECISION-MAKING

With your family or whatever decisions you have to make, when you've made the best decision possible, yet you know it's going to cause some pain—accept the pain but not the guilt. Sometimes, part of our head tries to make us feel guilty if we've made a decision that's been painful, not just for us, but maybe even for other people, yet it was the right decision. The key to accepting the pain but not the guilt—it's not pain that destroys you, it's guilt.

While you've been given some great ideas and strategies for nurturing your closest relationships, you still may be wondering how to strike the appropriate balance between your work and family life. This is a hot issue in our modern age, a topic on which everyone seems to have a strong opinion since everyone's personal situation is unique. We must resist easy answers to this dilemma and instead, I encourage you to embrace the challenge itself. While no perfect balance can ever be achieved, it is a battle we should fight until our dying day.

# Key phrase: In decision-making, accept the pain but not the guilt.

## BALANCING ACTS

Everybody's dilemma is the struggle between our own pursuits and others' expectations. For example, a woman is married to a baseball player who is gone most of the time. Would that be the ideal marriage? And the answer, certainly not. But should a man follow his talent and his unusual skills, he probably says yes. She says, well, at times I wish he was a banker and not a home run hitter. It's a dilemma for many of us. How to balance it all, making sure we don't sacrifice some values for others. It's difficult for two people to grow at the same rate. One becomes ambitious and one is a little more, let's say at home. How do you balance that and make it work? It's never-ending in terms of challenge.

A woman who has a career and children and husband and social responsibilities and friends and church and whatever faces big challenges daily. My current heroes are single mothers and school teachers. Teachers who have the patience to work with kids and try to get the message across and do a good job have my highest admiration. A single mother raising children is probably one of the toughest jobs in the world. She has to balance at-home work, a job, raise the kids, making sure that spiritually, personally, and socially they're okay. It seems almost impossible, but human beings have the unique ability to do the impossible. They make it work.

I've heard many, many stories about mothers who for years and years scrubbed floors or had other menial work to put her kids through college, and now those kids are professionals and credits to society.

Les Brown is one who has a great story (see www.lesbrown. com). He had a mama who really cared and did menial work until he got going and could help. We look at some people's lives and wonder, *How do they do that? How did they get through those tough breaks?* Sometimes we feel a little pressed wondering how we can balance career and fortune and all that. Hey, try scrubbing floors to put your kids through college. Then we think, *Hey, my problems are pretty simple and easy compared to what others may be experiencing.*

But we all have the push and pull. A woman wants a hero and a successful husband. She says, "Go conquer the world and be home by five o'clock." He thinks, *Wow. Let's see. How do I do that? Would she be happy with half the world? If I conquered just half the world and got home by six, would that be okay?* Let's all do a little compromising. Life is challenging—a balancing act.

# 9

# REASONS, DREAMS, AND GOALS

**N**ow that you have been presented the foundational philosophies and principles for turning any area of your life around, and you have strategies for three specific areas of your life, next you are ready to begin designing your future with my goal-setting workshop. Before beginning the actual workshop, the following are some key foundational ideas to set the stage for what is sure to be a life-changing activity for you.

Let's talk about setting goals. Not long after I first met Earl Shoaff, he asked me, "Mr. Rohn, maybe here's one of the best ways I can help you. Let me see your current list of goals and let's go over them and talk about them. I have the experience to help you.

"I don't have a list."

He said, "Wow, you don't have a list of your goals?"

"No."

He said, "Well, if you don't have a list of your goals, I can guess your bank balance within a few hundred dollars."

Which he did. "You mean if I had a list of goals, it would change my bank balance?"

He said, "Drastically."

That got my attention and all those years ago I learned how to set goals.

*The promise of the future is an awesome force.* We *look back* for experience, but we have to *look forward* now for inspiration.

Think about what gives you inspiration to get up in the morning and do your job, learn skills, develop all that you can possibly be is the promise of the future—and it can be so powerful that it can overwhelm any adversary and any difficulties you might have.

Here's a key phrase, reasons make the difference in how your life works out. Reasons make the difference in your appetite and zest for taking on the challenge, doing the job, and becoming successful.

# Key phrase: Reasons make the difference in how your life works out.

Mr. Shoaff said, "If you have enough reasons, you can do the most incredible things. You can get through the most difficult day. You can overcome the most unbelievable challenges if you have enough reasons. If you don't have a list of your goals, Mr. Rohn, it's probably because you don't have enough reasons."

He said, "Since I've met you, I'm sure you have enough intelligence. You have enough good health. You have many things working for you, but now you must work on having enough reasons, looking into the future, developing reasons for your goals."

## DEVELOP ENOUGH REASONS

We are primarily affected by:

*1. Environment,* which includes the political environment, social environment, and physical environment. Environment is whatever surrounds us, affects us—the city, the country, the countryside, the neighborhood, the office, the people. We're constantly affected and shaped by our reactions and decision-making. A lot of our reasoning depends on the environment and especially our physical environment. We need to pay attention and make every contribution we can to make our and everyone's environment welcoming. It's one small planet.

Remember those first and subsequent pictures from space? Looking back on Earth, it looked so fragile, so small. I thought, *Wow, so many people live here. How can that be? We must take care of it.* Right now, it's the only planet we have. Let's do everything we can to be responsible.

**2. *Events.*** Some events affect all of us. Some affect the world regionally, nationally, or by state or community, but some events affect us all. Events that affect all of us include wars and the weather. Other more specific and personal events include weddings, promotions, births, vacations, and work-related duties.

**3. *What we know.*** We're affected by what we know and what we don't know. The accumulation of knowledge or the lack of knowledge affects your dreams, affects your future, affects your income, affects your bank account, affects your associations—everything. You have to be a life-long student. No matter your age, study so you can learn how to make wise decisions that will give you the best chance to build a better future.

**4. *Results.*** We're affected by results. Whatever your current economic results, whatever projects you've launched, the results up until now affect you. All the results you've experienced in the past until now have affected you, your decision-making, your attitude. Learn to use results—good or bad—to your benefit.

**5. *Dreams.*** We're affected by our dreams. Our dreams, meaning the view of our future. It's important to ensure that the greatest pull on your life is the pull of a better future. Some people let the past pull them back, like gravity. They live in the past. They live in the mistakes and discouragements of the past. To their detriment, they allow the past to affect their future. Look only in the past to learn from your mistakes to launch you into the future—look ahead to a better day.

Dreams and goals can become magnets; the stronger the goal, the higher the purpose, the more powerful the objective, and the stronger the magnet pulls you in that direction. Not only do your goals and your objectives pull you in the right direction, they also pull you through all kinds of down days and difficult times. Dreams and goals will pull you through the winters of your life.

Some people get lost in the confusion of the day simply because their goal is not bright enough to pull them through. One writer of ancient times wrote that "we can walk through the valley even though there are shadows of death." And why is it possible to walk through the valley even though there's death and shadows and difficulties? Because we have a view of the other side of the valley.

# Key phrase:
# Dreams and goals are magnets pulling you toward a better life.

## ALWAYS HAVE GOALS

When you've accomplished some goals, you need some more to accomplish. It's very important when you reach a goal that's significant or important to you, it's time to celebrate. Celebrate significant and not-so-significant accomplishments. If it's important to you, it doesn't have to be world-changing or life-changing. If it's a goal that's really important to you, and you finally reached it, celebrate!

Hopefully on your list of goals you had some family goals; and if the family together finally reaches a goal, celebrate with the family. And if you're checking it off the list, let each member of the family put their check mark on this accomplished goal too because the whole family worked on it. This will help each member of your family want to make a longer list of goals or a list of their own. Wow, think what else we could do—what they could do personally.

The same is true of you individually. When you accomplish something, check it off the list, celebrate. Celebration creates excitement to develop a longer list.

You also need ongoing goals. When the early astronauts went to the moon, some of them who returned had psychological problems. Some drank too much and got into other difficulties. Why? One of the reasons is because after such a life, nation, and worldwide accomplishment, where does a person go from there? To help avoid the void, after later voyages, astronauts who returned from the moon were assigned numerous projects to keep them busy. And the same is true of you and me. After you've reached your goals, make another list. After you've reached those, make another list.

As mentioned previously, my father lived to be 93 years old. You can't imagine the goals he had. One of his goals when he was 92 was to get his driver's license renewed. Guess what? He got it renewed for four years. At 92 he was telling people, "Got my driver's license renewed for four years," and he'd show his driver's license around to everybody. Unbelievable.

Set goals to replace goals that you've achieved on and on, the rest of your life. How far should you go? As far as you can. How many books should you read? As many as you can. How many friends should you make? As many as you can. How much should you earn? As much as you can. What should you try to be? All you possibly can.

The purpose of the following goal-setting workshop exercise is to stretch you, get you to think, get you to wonder, get you to ponder. *I wonder what might be possible?*

# 10

# GOALS-SETTING WORKSHOP

The following workshop section is the same goal-setting workshop I presented at exclusive weekend seminars over the years. I recommend you read and complete this activity in a place that is quiet and where you will not be interrupted. It is also recommended that you bracket out enough time so you can complete the workshop in one sitting.

You'll need a pad of paper, a pen, and a megadose of curiosity. So if you're ready, let's begin!

During this workshop, I'm asking a series of questions, which will serve you as well as provide a model you can teach your children, you can teach in classes, you can teach anywhere.

I give you the question first, and then I recommend you take time to work on the exercise. So read the question and then work on the exercise. If for lack of time, you have to stop working on the exercise before finishing, you can continue later. But please make sure you follow through with each exercise on setting goals—because I think it's so valuable.

## 1. WHAT FIVE THINGS HAVE YOU ALREADY ACCOMPLISHED THAT YOU'RE PROUD OF?

Give yourself some credit before you go to work on the future. I'm sure you've had accomplishments in the past. Think about them and make a list. I encourage you to take time right now to list five things you've already accomplished, that you're proud of.

(When you're working with kids, this part of the exercise is important as well. Ask them what five things they accomplished that made them feel proud. Sometimes you may have to make suggestions such as sports, school, whatever. When working with others, part of the format is to do a little coaching to help people understand what is being requested.)

## 2. WHAT DO YOU WANT IN THE NEXT 10 YEARS?

I want you to make a list of at least 50. Don't list what you think you can get—this is a list of what you want. If everything fell into place and you could have anything you wanted over the next 10 years, what would be on that list? Don't list something you think you can earn, or you can buy, or think you can finally be so successful you can get. List what you really want for yourself during the next 10 years.

When you start writing your list, make one long list down the left side of the paper (not side by side but one underneath the other). If any on your list is private, put it in code so nobody can figure it out if they saw your list. Let your dreams run free—not what you think you can get but what you want if everything fell into place and you could have whatever you wanted over the next 10 years, what would that be? Little things, major things, insignificant things, doesn't matter. Just make the list.

Maybe your list will include places you want to visit, experiences you would like to have. Parachute out of an airplane, star in a movie, play in a band. Win an Olympic gold medal. Start a family. Some changes you'd like to make, some habits you'd like to drop, some new ones you'd like to acquire. You might make a list of the people you want to meet over the next 10 years. A cabin in the mountains, a maid, a cook, a chauffeur. How about your investments, properties?

What would really do it for you? Become a wine connoisseur. I'm learning more and more how to make wine. It's an interesting process. A hobby you'd like to start, collecting. New car, become a race driver. Skills you want to help teach your children. I taught my girls how to swim, how to dive. Such great satisfaction when they used to say, "Watch me, Daddy, watch me. Look how good I am. You taught me. Watch me." Make a contribution to society. Make a contribution to your community.

Please pause your reading right now and begin making that list.

## 3. GIVE EACH ITEM A TIMEFRAME.

Now I want you to look at each item on your list and give each a number that reflects how long you think it would take to make to achieve that goal. Just estimate if it may take 1 or 3 or 5 or 10 years. Doesn't have to be exact. If less than one year, just make it a year. If more than 10, just make it 10 or 10 plus.

Please stop reading and do this part of the exercise now.

## 4. COUNT THE "YEARS."

Now go back over the number of years you assigned to your "wants" and count them, how many ones, how many threes, how many fives, how many tens, and then make a list of those numbers. For example:

- Travel around the world – 5 years
- Learn to speak Italian – 1 year
- Become a master chef – 5 years
- Enlarge my business worldwide – 10 plus
- Number of Years
- 2 – 5 years
- 1 – 1 year
- 1 – 10 plus

Please pause your reading and complete this exercise.

## 5. PRIORITIZE.

Look over your list of one-year goals, which are the four most important? Pick out the four most important and number them in priority order.

The process of goal setting is what turned me on at age 25—*goals for accomplishment and personal progress*. Once the fires were lit for me, they have never been extinguished. Since I was 25 years old, no one has ever said to me, "When are you going to get going? When are you going to get off the couch? When are you going to make something of yourself?" I've never heard that since I was 25, now I have it all taken care of. What I've heard after turning 25: "When are you going to slow down? You've visited how many countries? You're working too hard." Amazing.

I can't say it strongly enough. It's easy to get lazy in designing the day and designing the year and designing the future and designing what you want to accomplish—and just cross your fingers and hope it'll all work out, that the favorable winds will blow it all your way. I'm telling you, it's not going to happen that way.

The way I kept my focus was to teach what I learned. I didn't need recognition. I just wanted to share my good fortune with others so they could do the same. Just go give everybody you can think of the keys to success, and your own self-satisfaction is recognition enough. If they never put a crown on your head, who cares?

Please stop now and identify the most important top four, 1-year items on your list. When you complete the exercise, resume reading.

## 6. ANSWER "WHY" THOSE FOUR GOALS ARE IMPORTANT.

This step will take a little bit of time. Think about each of the four and why those four goals are important to you. The "why" is very important, and I'll give you more information on that upcoming. But for now, write a brief paragraph about why those four goals are significant to you.

Please take time to write those brief explanations now.

# Key phrase: Without a strong "why," the "how" may seem to too difficult to accomplish.

When the "why" gets stronger, the "how" gets easier. So how do you manage your time? If you have strong and powerful enough goals, you'll figure out how to manage your time, you'll read a book on the subject, you'll do something about it. If it's not worth it, why would you bother studying the art of managing your time if it really doesn't matter? But if it really matters to accomplish your goals and why you want to accomplish them, you can do anything you need to do.

You can get up any hour, read any book, take any class, make any change, develop any skill, do any discipline. You can do it all. When the why starts to grow, the how gets simple. Maybe one of your goals is to have a million-dollar home on the hill overlooking Snake River Valley. Okay. That'd be a good goal.

Next questions: Why? What for? A house is a house is a house. A million-dollar home would be nice, even wonderful, but what for? Purpose is stronger than the object. The object would be the house and that'll pull you toward the goal. And that's a worthy goal to go for, the object of the house.

But a stronger goal is the *purpose* for the million-dollar home. You say, "Well, it'll be the centerpiece of all the family's activity with all kinds of unique people coming and going and the influence and things will happen in this place." See, now we're getting somewhere.

# Key phrase:
# Purpose is stronger than the object.

That's one of my best pieces of advice for the whole chapter. Purpose is stronger than the object. It's okay to have plenty of objects to go for on your goal list but always keep asking yourself the question and sometimes it's good to write it out. "Here's why I want this money. Here's why I want this place. Here's why." Start developing those reasons, and the goal starts to become incredibly powerful and motivating.

Some of your goals should be regarding personal development, the person you wish to become. Develop skills that make you attractive to the marketplace. Develop the temperament and the attitude that makes you attractive to the business world, the attitude and the temperament that makes you a splendid spouse and parent. Study the art of becoming because it's not the stuff you accumulate that makes you valuable—it's what you become that makes you valuable. I keep saying this year after year—your value is in the person you become.

I admired my friend Mark Hughes for the fortune he made and the company he built. Guess what I admired more? The person he became in a short 44 years. He was unique. He bought the idea at age 19 of personal development and worked on it daily from that day until the time he died. The idea of becoming an attractive person, a skillful person, a good friend, a good colleague, a good partner, a good member of the Round Table, a contributor. Those are the keys to becoming a reputable, successful, and valuable person.

All of what I'm telling you changed my life, altered the course of my life—from milking cows to sitting on a platform speaking to thousands of people every year. Incredible. What a great journey.

## 7. WHAT KIND OF PERSON MUST I BECOME TO ACHIEVE ALL I WANT?

For the next exercise, I want you to take time to look at and review the whole list that you've written and the exercises you've completed. Now I want you to answer this question: What kind of person must I become to achieve all I want? Take all the time you need to write down that answer now. What kind of person must I become to achieve all I want?

When you have completed that exercise, resume reading.

## 8. WHAT IS YOUR CONCEPT OF THE PERSON YOU THINK YOU MUST BECOME TO ACHIEVE WHAT YOU WANT?

Now you have two scenarios working together: *What you become helps you achieve—and what you achieve helps you become.* Likewise, the more you become, the more you can achieve and the more you achieve, the more you can become. Who knows which affects the other the most, but there is definitely a correlation. So start by writing a few sentences. Your concept of the person you think you must become to achieve what you want. This is time for a little truth here.

Maybe you need to become much wiser than you are at the moment. Or you need to become stronger. Maybe you need to improve your health habits—eat less and exercise more. Maybe you need a little coaching: physical coaching, spiritual coaching, developing skills coaching. To be the influence you want to be. You have to build an incredible reputation. Ask yourself, *What kind of person must I be to attract all that I want in my life and the people I want and the opportunities that I want?* When you knock on the door, an opportunity opens, you must stand there as a confident and well-groomed person, or you may not be invited in.

One of the most mysterious and unique phrases of Jesus was when He said, "I stand at the door and knock." If you opened the door, would you have invited Him in, this extraordinary person? You say, "Wow. Yeah, of course." Then He said, "If you invite me, I'll come in, and sit down, and talk things over with you." Are you that kind of attractive person that if you knocked on the door of opportunity and it opened and you stood there, would you be the kind of person whom opportunity would say, "Come right in and sit down and let's talk about the future"? Yes, you definitely want to be that kind of person.

## THE SIMPLE APPROACH TO LIFE AND SUCCESS

Now that you have set your goals for the future, you have a blueprint for your life. *Any day, including today, can be the day that turns your life around.* To accomplish your goals as quickly as possible, I recommend you simplify your life and your thinking as much as possible. That's what this session is all about. While there seems to be no end to the stream of success approaches and systems available, I urge you to resist complex new answers to age-old problems. Save your hard thinking for your goal achievement and take the simple approach to success.

I usually take the simple approach to life when trying to figure it out or trying to comprehend it. And I believe humor and wit go a long way to that simple approach. Sometimes it's best to return silly for silly. A little wit helps to disarm all the stuff that you don't want to take responsibility for. For an example, Lady Astor in the English Parliament was exasperated with Churchill and she said, "Winston Churchill, if you were my husband, I would put poison in your coffee." And Churchill responded, "Lady Astor, if you were my wife, I would drink it."

A few simple ideas can be life-changing, whether it's economic or health. My mama said, "You don't have to radically change." She recommended that I eat an apple a day. I said, "Well, can I have some candy?" She said, "Yes, if you have the candy *and* the apple, but not the candy as the substitute for the apple." See, that made sense to me. Okay, I can have candy if I also eat an apple. She said it in such a simple way. I understood.

Shoaff, my mentor in business, had the same unique style. When I said, "Hey, things cost too much," he said, "No, you can't afford them." Immediately I thought, *That's a new way to look at the circumstance.*

More than once he showed me alternate ways to look at things. One day he said, "Why aren't you doing better?"

I showed him my paycheck and said, "This is all the company pays."

He said, "Well, that's not true."

"Yes it is, this is my check."

He says, "No, Mr. Rohn, this is all that the company pays *you.* This is not all that the company pays."

In just two or three simple sentences, he opened a whole new world of consciousness to think about. He says, "Don't some people in the same company earn four or five times this amount that you're getting?"

"Well, yes."

He said, "Well, then this is not all that the company pays. And if you were four or five times more valuable than you are now, do you think your paycheck would multiply by four or five?"

"Yes, I guess it would."

He said, "Why don't we go to work on that?"

Lesson learned—you don't have to work on the company to pay you more money. You only have to work on yourself to become more valuable.

Simple ways of saying things so simply. It doesn't have to be radical or complicated. The key is just to start. For instance, if in sales, start making three presentations a day in a year, which makes a thousand. A thousand seems like too many, but just start is easy, then continue and do not yield to the temptation to slack off and return to old habits that take you nowhere.

## LITTLE THINGS MAKE A BIG DIFFERENCE

My mama taught me the little things. Pick up after yourself, don't leave your trash on the floor. A little thing like that I remember. I got a toothpick once at the cafe and I took the little cellophane off the toothpick and dropped it on the floor. Mama said, "No, no, you wouldn't do that at home. Just pick it up and put it in your pocket, then when you get home, put it in the trash."

And somebody says, "Well, what difference does that make? The little cellophane on the toothpick?" Here's what makes the difference. *The habit makes the difference* primarily for you but also for the café worker who would have to pick it up. A small contribution to the overall environment will give you the incredible feeling of self-worth because you have good habits. That's the real deal—embracing good habits that last a lifetime.

How about the habit of turning out the lights at home when you're not in the room? Or when you're going to check out of your hotel, you turn off the room lights before you leave. These are small contributions, habits. But if everybody did that, the energy demands and costs would lessen dramatically. Someone says, "Well, the hotel gets the benefit." Hey, it doesn't matter who gets the benefit. Guess what's the greatest benefit? Being a person of unique habits. Habits that not only make you perform as far as skills are concerned, but habits that make you feel good about yourself.

And then sometimes we get the question, *Why do it?* And the best answer to that is, *Why not do it?* Why not do all the easy things that make a contribution? Open the door for an elderly person, or any person. Motion a pedestrian to proceed across the street. Allow a mother with a toddler to go in front of you in line at the grocery store. Who knows what the total contribution could be if we all used good manners and thought of others before ourselves? Even if no one else has good habits, if you do and I do, it makes us better human beings. It makes us feel better about ourselves and the people we do nice things for feel better too.

I presented a television series and the title of the talk was "Things My Mother Taught Me." Many found it very interesting. The following are some of the wisdom my mother shared with me and now me to you. I encourage you to absorb some of this wisdom for yourself.

THE DAY THAT TURNS YOUR LIFE AROUND

Mother taught me to always eat before I attended a banquet so I wouldn't appear hungry when I arrived. Then I could do what is most important—socialize. So rather than go to the banquet to make up for a meal you haven't had and eat everything in sight, not having any time to socialize and mingle with the people, take Mama's advice, "Always eat before you go to a banquet or dinner party." That's really good advice. Little things she taught me added up to a lot of good common sense.

What else did Mama say? "Sit up straight." She said that because she had a vision of me sitting up straight, shoulders back, chin down, look up, look everyone in the eye. Good posture. Feel good about yourself and other people will feel good about you. Our parents' vision of who they wanted us to be gave us those little tips. Who was it that wrote the book, *Everything I Needed to Know I Learned in Kindergarten?* Robert Fulghum, thank you.

Some countries of the world show unique respect. When I visit Mexico, they don't just say, "Hello, Jim Rohn." They say, "Hello, Mr. Jim Rohn." It's just part of the custom. "This is Mr. Jim Rohn."

When I first visited southern states in the US, I remember even as a kid people would say, "Yes ma'am. Yes sir. No sir." Where I was raised, we really didn't do that as a routine. But I like it. It shows respect.

There are many nuances in life that we can learn to help make our lives better, help make the world better, help people feel good about themselves, and feel good about us. Incredible. So consider your environment, whatever little thing you can think of that gives you pride and joy in doing to make a contribution. As small as it may seem, make it for what it does for the environment, for the people—and what it does for you. So keep working on your skills and habits to be the best you can possibly be.

I want to be the best I can possibly be at delivering the message of good words for those who attend my seminars and read my books. I work on it daily.

## CHALLENGES OF LONG-TERM GOAL SETTING

The same simple approach that my mother and mentor Earl Shoaff modeled for me spilled over into my entire success philosophy, a philosophy that has served me as well as the hundreds of thousands of seminar attendees over more than 40 years.

When asked to address the challenges of long-term goal setting in a world that is changing faster by the day, my response follows.

I make my long-term goals so simple that they don't really have complications. For instance, if on your goal list is to own a ranch in Montana and you say, "Well, if I worked hard and maybe it's my second year of following an entrepreneurial project and I'm doing fairly well, I think maybe I could accomplish that in five years. Sure enough, if good things happen, it's down to three years. If it takes me a little longer, maybe that's possible in 10 years, but I'll just leave it on my list and not make it an obsession. And then maybe the more I think about it, I may not want a farm in Montana, but rather an apartment in New York on Park Avenue. I think I'll change my goal to that."

Let that type of conversation in your mind inspire you.

If goals inspire you to higher achievements and occasions and places you want to visit and things you want to see and people you want to meet, even if only a little of it comes true—all of it served as inspiration along the way to do better and work harder. You can say, "Maybe some of these goals will be closer than I thought, now it looks exciting," all of that serves you well. Who cares how close you got? Who cares if you set 200 goals and only reached 10? It doesn't really matter.

## TAKE IT EASY ON YOURSELF

If you make it really easy on yourself, tear up the list if you want to. Start over. You may have some better information now. You may have learned more about a different more beneficial endeavor. How about setting another goal? I think that's the key. I made it easy on myself. Make a list of what you want and start checking off what is easy to get. There may be a lot of little things that you can start checking off, and then let the rest of it all unfold.

But you might as well dream about having an upstairs maid and a downstairs maid if you happen to visit a rich man's home and say, "Wow, that's the life for me. I'm going to put that on my list." The guy's got a limousine and a driver, you say, "Wow, someday that's for me," and then later you say, "No, this limousine and driver deal, that's not for me." But let it inspire you in the meantime. Why not? Even if you change your mind and throw that goal out, put another goal in.

One of my friends flew me on his Learjet from San Jose to Van Nuys, close to my home. I thought, *Wow, it'd be nice to have a jet like this*. But then I thought, *It only seats four people or five. It's really too small*. The friend also has an eight-passenger helicopter that seats a pilot and a copilot and six passengers. It's the latest state of the art. *Wow*, I thought. *But do I really need a helicopter? Not really.*

Then, I thought I'd like to live in a mansion and have all the stuff. But when I visited someone who has the mansion and the security and the servants and the groundskeepers, and the whole house seemed chaotic to me. We had a cup of coffee and when almost finished drinking it, someone came and took it away. With my temperament and style, I concluded, *This is really not the lifestyle for me. I want to live a more simple life.* But for someone else, a house full of servants and security and the whole entourage, that's for them.

It's okay to dream—and it's okay to change your mind too. Having my fishing line in a tranquil stream in Montana, that suits my style a little better. So give yourself a chance to go from luxury to simplicity, whatever. But at first, let your mind dream, *Wouldn't it be great to have this and that?* Make a list of all that stuff. Let it serve you well, even though along the way you change it all or throw most of it away.

At the peak of my giving seminars, I had 13 offices in cities in California. Tony Robbins ran one of my offices, started working for me when he was 17, managed one of my offices when he was 20. I presented a seminar in each city, in 13 cities a month. I had the elaborate entourage. It was an exciting and unbelievable time in my life.

One day I decided, *Someday I shall have no office, I shall have no secretary, I shall be free.* And sure enough, that day finally arrived. People ask me now, "What is your email address?" And I say, "I don't have one." I do have a website

**175**

that someone else runs, but I have really simplified my life. A company that I do a lot of business with around the world asked me, "Do you want an office?" I said, "No." He said, "Do you want a secretary?" I said, "No."

Then I did say once, "Yes, I'm going to have a satellite connection and put a fax machine in my motor home so that I can be in touch, but out of reach. I want somebody to say, 'Yes, you can contact him, but you can't find him for a while. He's not gone forever but he's gone for a while.'"

I do seek solitude, chances to get away. My farm in Idaho overlooking Snake River is a great place to get away and deal in agriculture and build a few homes, a little change of pace from flying around the world for speaking engagements. It's exciting for me, but for now, I have no office and no secretary and no email address. I've managed to escape most of it. Sometimes, you just have to make hard and fast decisions.

I've worked hard to walk the talk and simplify my life—while at the same time expanding opportunities for greater success, wealth, and happiness. It can be done. Success can be simple.

## HERITAGES

The following is the summary of one of my classic speeches, "Today, I am a Wealthy Man." In it, you'll discover that the path to real wealth can be found in several simple things that everyone possesses, but too often take for granted.

Although I say I'm a wealthy man, this speech doesn't have much to do with money—yet very wealthy I am indeed. Read on.

## I'M WEALTHY BECAUSE OF MY FAMILY HERITAGE.

Because of my parents and my grandparents. My grandmother studied nutrition, passed it on to my mother. Back in those days when my mother studied and practiced good nutrition, she was called a "health nut" for studying the benefits of vitamins. Mama used to mix up some of this stuff for me and Papa and say, "If this don't kill us, I think it'll help"—as we were gagging this stuff down.

Because of the practice and study of better nutrition her doctor told her that she extended her life at least 20 years. He said, "When your mother died, the walls of her heart were paper thin. How she lived these last 20 years is incomprehensible." I told him about Mama's commitment to healthy nutrition, vitamins, and juices. My father lived to be 93 and never had a major illness. I've never had one either and this has been passed on to my children, my grandchildren.

My family heritage. What's that worth? It's worth a fortune. Contemplate every once in a while on your blessings, and part of your blessing is your heritage.

## I'M WEALTHY BECAUSE OF MY COUNTRY HERITAGE.

Those of us who come from free countries can engage in enterprise to start with a dollar and make a fortune, even become a millionaire. What value is that heritage? It's priceless. We enjoy the benefit of courts of justice that we didn't establish. We enjoy the benefit of laws we didn't create. We enjoy the benefit of learning institutions we didn't found. We enjoy the benefit of medicine we didn't discover. Heritage history is a gift in so many ways.

## I'M WEALTHY BECAUSE OF MY EXPERIENCES.

Experience makes you rich. You must treat your experiences as high-value commodities. You must treat your experiences as capital so that you can invest in the future, which you've learned about throughout the book. My experiences have taken me around the world. For example, a group got together last year to celebrate my birthday. It was one of the most unbelievable experiences of my life. We were in Italy and they gave me a helicopter tour of Sorento, Naples, Vesuvius, the Isle of Capri, and Pompeii from the air. Wow. I've enjoyed extraordinary experiences.

## I'M WEALTHY BECAUSE OF MY FRIENDS.

Friendship is one of the greatest wealths of all. Those wonderful people who know all about you and still like you. Friends. I just lost a friend; David died about three years ago. He is the one I mentioned in a previous chapter. The one I said that if I was stuck in a foreign jail accused unduly, if they would allow me one phone call, I would've called David. Why would I call him? He would've come and rescued me. End of story. That's who you call friend. Somebody who would come and get you.

## I'M WEALTHY BECAUSE OF WHAT I'VE LEARNED.

I'm wealthy from what people have taught me, from the Earl Shoaffs of the world and from other people who have made contributions to my intellectual discovery, who have helped me refine the track I live on for good health, for prosperity, for all the things valuable. We can't put a price tag on someone's book or someone's conversation that added to your knowledge. Someone who gives you wisdom when you need it the most, when you can't think of the ideas, when your head is so clouded, maybe with despair and the clouds of difficulty hover near, this is when you need somebody to whisper valuable information in your ear that helps you to survive and then go on to succeed.

What is that knowledge worth? You can't put a price tag on it. What's a seminar worth? You can't put a price tag on it. The actual cost of a seminar pays for the lights and the room and somebody like me to come and speak and the staff and all the other things—but the price of the knowledge and the people you meet can't be calculated.

You can't put a price tag on ideas. That would be impossible. If you read a book that spares you from having a heart attack, what would it be worth? Someone says "$19.95." I say, "No, no. That's the cost of the book. That's what it costs for the cover and the ink and the pages and the words and getting it to you and the brokers and all that stuff in between. That's the $20. You can't pay for the ideas. They're free."

A key thing I've learned, never begrudge the money you spend on personal education. If you keep developing your mind and your perception and your awareness and your ability to discover, the fortune is yours. The health is yours. The promise is yours. A good family relationship is yours. Friendship is yours. Everything is yours. If you continue to accelerate your education, it's the best way to invest your money—in your personal self-education.

## I'M WEALTHY BECAUSE OF MY FUTURE.

You can't believe the number of people who ask me, "Jim Rohn, what do you want to do in the future? You have the wealth and the resources to do anything you want to do. What do you want to do?" Do you know how unbelievable that question is? My future is mine to create—thanks to the day that turned my life around!

## I'M WEALTHY BECAUSE OF UNIQUE LOVE EXPERIENCES.

I told you about Judy. That was a unique experience for me, even when we parted. Her two sons whom I inherited as stepsons are now part of my family; my two daughters and these two sons are very close. Judy's ex-husband and I are best friends. That's kind of unique. But it was one of the great experiences of my life. A major share of what I am today came from that unique experience of a love affair, unmatched.

# 11

# LET'S GO TOGETHER

The statement, "Let's go do it," is infinitely more powerful than "I'm going to do it." Truly, no one is an island. We are all interdependent and can dramatically increase our chances for personal transformation by utilizing the wisdom and guidance of others who have been down the path before us.

That's what the concept of mentoring is all about. Since mentors played such a big role in the day that turned my life around, this chapter discusses my major mentors and the incredible personal qualities they possess. These ideas can be helpful for you as you either search for your own mentor or as you mentor others.

## MENTORS AND THEIR INFLUENCE

I wasn't searching for a mentor, but one just sort of fell in my lap. A friend of mine said, "You have got to meet this guy I'm working for, Earl Shoaff. He's rich, but he's easy to talk to. He's got a unique philosophy of life and business." I say, "Okay.

Yeah, I'll meet him." I met him and he invited me to join him in his business and he became my mentor.

Right away I got the sense that he delighted just as much in other people's success as he did his own. That caught my attention immediately. And he had the ability to look into the future and see the possibilities that I couldn't see. I can't remember how often he said, "Trust me. I'm telling you, trust me. Here's how it will go if you'll stay steady and do it right." That was great mentoring.

Then, there was Bill Bailey. We had been associated in business and projects for many, many years. Bill's unique in that he can read a 200-page book in about 20 minutes, and then tell you about the book, making it more interesting than if you read it yourself. His life experiences spanned from performing Shakespeare to a boxing career, time spent in the Navy, and a business career of wealth and productivity—he is one of those larger-than-life characters. It's been my good fortune to know him all these years.

One night on the second bottle of wine while down on our goat farm in Kentucky where we're in business together, Bill and I waxed eloquent. He's a great conversationalist. I ask a question, and he poses some possibilities that I never thought of. And I'm sure I do the same for him. It's great to have that kind of interchange, where you kind of wonder together about things. "This could be a possibility. This could be an answer. Who knows?" He's also written poetry that's unique, and his studies and his concepts are valuable for me. But best of all is simply the friendship, the chance to get together. Not just to share ideas but to enjoy unique life experiences.

My parents were my unique mentors. My father was remarkable in his bit of philosophy. He said, "Always do more than you get paid for to make an investment in your future." That's a pretty good seminar in itself. My mother was more of a reader and a scholar, and taught me well, gave me a great foundation. Primarily, they gave me a great place to live and learn and grow. And I always had the sense that when I did leave home, no matter what happened I could always go home. So out in the world if things didn't go my way my attitude was, "You better treat me right. I can go home. Who needs this." Not to be arrogant, but I had bold confidence that no matter how things turned out, whether it turned out right or went upside-down, my mom and dad would welcome me home.

My parents' relationship was really special; it was great between them for 65-plus years of marriage. They gave me an incredible sense of security and caring. That whether I did it right, or did it wrong, or somewhere between, it really didn't matter. Home was always a place I could rest and think things through, work it out, and then go back and conquer the rest of the world. See what I can do. There's really not much better sense of security than that.

My parents have passed on now, but their lingering influence of my growing-up years plus the security and tranquility and sense of refuge from a busy world gave me such a great start in life. And knowing that they truly loved me when I was rich and when I was poor, broke, struggling, and when I did well. They enjoyed my success, the applause, and the experiences of being recognized.

I would wish the same kind of experience for everyone. So I counsel parents to the best of my ability to provide that kind of security and framework for their children. That they feel comfortable even though they misstep, cross the line, get in trouble, upside-down. If a kid gets in trouble, guess who he wants to call? His mother. They think, *She'll come and get me. Papa may say to the sheriff, "Well, leave him in jail over-night to teach him a lesson." But not Mama. No. If she's there, she'll come and get me.*

## PERFECTION IS OVERRATED

Quite often the concept of mentoring is mistakenly associated with perfection. People look for the perfectly well-rounded individual with few, if any, character defects to be their mentor. As a result of this unrealistic expectation, a person can be continually let down by the person they formerly admired. I advise you to abandon an unrealistic search for perfection in a mentor and instead learn from both their strengths and weaknesses.

It's hard to find a mentor who has all the exact qualities you may want. If you want someone to mentor you in good health, spirituality, business, and career, and relationships—it's doubtful if you will find it all in one package, one person. But genius comes in strange packages sometimes, along with their idiosyncrasies. If we lived during the time of some of the geniuses of the past, we would be surprised, no doubt. Leonardo da Vinci may have been impossible to live with. But he was an incredible genius.

So sometimes you have to look past the idiosyncrasies and faults, and not so much at the strange package that a mentor comes in, appreciate the person and what he or she can contribute to your life's journey. Unless it's totally intolerable, of course.

Be prepared to tolerate inconsistencies of remarkable people who have much to share. Take for example my friend and my mentor, Earl Shoaff. He drank champagne every day and he smoked Camels. He wasn't a chain smoker but pretty close, back when the packages didn't say, "These things will kill you." So, he smoked his Camels and drank his champagne, and on those choices he miscalculated. For all of his other wisdom and uniqueness, he just didn't have any concept that they were going to kill him.

At age 49, his miscalculations taught me as well. Look at the whole of life and make sure you're not a bit disillusioned by something that can someday shorten your life, or do you in, or wreck your enterprise, or disengage your marriage, or whatever. Keep looking at everything. Carelessness and casualness sometimes create casualties, both on the freeway and in business, marriage, and friendship.

My giving advice started long ago, when I said, "Be a student, not a follower." I mentioned in one of my seminars, "I seek no disciples." I'm not looking for a following. I just want

# Key phrase:
# Carelessness and casualness may create casualties.

to find people who want to share good ideas, come together, let me share my experiences and see if it's valuable.

Personally, I would never be so enamored by someone as to make them an idol and make myself a disciple. I would not do that. On the radical side, this relationship can cause trouble, even death. You could wind up in a fire in Waco, Texas, like David Koresh and his followers. That's the radical extreme. Use a mentor not as an idol or a hero, but as a source of important information. And if fortunately, like me, they become good friends, that's an added bonus.

## MENTORING SKILLS

There are specific skills that I developed to mentor others and consequently, become successful in my network marketing business. You can use the following information to mentor an individual or a team to outstanding levels of success that they never thought they were capable of.

These skills and developing a new life philosophy changed my life forever.

***The first skill I learned that changed my life was how to get a customer and make a sale.*** When sharing a product, talk about its merits, persuade someone that it's the best, and they agree to buy—that's the simple art of sales. We're not talking high-powered spacecraft technical skills here. It's simply sharing something you've discovered with someone else and doing it well enough so they agree to participate.

When I learned to sell, my income multiplied by five. Now, it didn't take much to do that because I wasn't doing that well in farm country. But it did multiply my income by five. Sales, getting customers, laying that incredible foundation for an entrepreneurial career was the start. So now I had two skills—milking cows and making sales.

*The next skill I learned that changed me forever was recruiting*—introducing the business opportunity to new people. Learning how to give a good invitation. Learning how to give two kinds of presentation, formal and informal. And the third part of recruiting, of course, is following up.

When you start a new life, you have to take care of it, like a new mother takes care of her baby. You don't start a new life and then abandon it. No. You start a new life and nourish it like a mother and protect it like a father. You have to be both mother and father to a new recruit. Nourishment, ideas, and protection help defend your new life against the encroachment of outside negative voices.

## SPONSORSHIP

In this art of recruiting, we call follow-up as being a sponsor, which is like being a bridge. You are helping someone move from darkness to light, from skeptic to faith, from not knowing to knowing, from no confidence in themselves to gaining confidence. You're the bridge that helps people emerge from the shadows into the sunlight.

Being a sponsor is one of the most exciting positions to occupy in all of the network marketing industry. It is the bridge to help people cross the bridge from discouragement to recognition. That's what recruiting is all about. You have the answers. They've been looking for the answers. You see something in them before they can see it in themselves. You assure them that it's possible to be more than they are. There-fore, they can earn more and have more.

I believe that this is one of the great arts in the world, and here's what's exciting about this art—it pays big money because now you operate a unique philosophy taught first in the Bible. The question was asked, "How can we achieve greatness?" Great wealth, great power, great influence, great recognition, great self-esteem. "How can we achieve great-ness," the master teacher was asked. And he revealed his formula for achieving personal greatness, saying, "Find a way to serve the many, for service to many leads to greatness," for those who are interested. Some people aren't interested. But for those who are, service to many leads to greatness.

Someone says, "Well, the best I can do is just take care of myself." Which is okay, but it doesn't lead to greatness. Some-one else says, "I have enough bills of my own. I can't worry about someone else's bills." That's okay too, but it doesn't lead to greatness. Greatness is helping people pay their bills, and you forget about yours. Because if you help enough people pay theirs, yours disappear. Help people with problems, your problems disappear. The key to greatness, the master teacher taught, is finding a way. Now, a lot of people would like to serve many people, but they don't have a way. And what's exciting about you and your business—you now have the way!

## IT'S UP TO YOU

Whether you use it or not is up to you. Whether you cash it in or not is up to you. Whether you make a fortune or just a little, that's all up to you. It's the same marketing, the same product, the same everything for everybody. The marketing system is the same. The difference is each person's philosophy and each person's individual ambition.

Whatever your ambitions are, now you have the ways and means to serve as many people as you would like. This is what's exciting about recruiting. Now that you're involved, you can directly and indirectly affect the lives of dozens of people. You can directly and indirectly affect the lives of hundreds of people, even thousands of people. And the pay rises accordingly. If you affect a few, you earn that pay. If you affect the many, you earn that pay. But the secret is found in the Bible. Service to many leads to greatness.

President John F. Kennedy said in his inaugural speech, in essence, "Don't ask what people can do for you. Don't ask what the country can do for you. Don't ask what the government can do for you. Rather, ask what you can do for others and for your country." Ask yourself, *What could I do for the people? Can I earn trophies, recognition, self-esteem by serving people? Will serving people give me a chance to make a fortune? Could I directly and indirectly serve many people in my country?* If you participate in the philosophy and steps provided in this book, the answer is yes.

## GIVE PEOPLE WHAT THEY WANT

Zig Ziglar and I have been good friends for a lot of years. Zig said, "Money isn't everything, but it ranks right up there with oxygen." Zig is right. Zig also said, "My dentist told me, 'Zig, only floss the teeth you want to keep. Forget the rest.'" But Zig is famous for this philosophy statement that goes right along with the Bible and John Kennedy: "If you help enough people get what they want, you can have everything you want."

Wanting everything you want is called self-interest. But it's okay to have self-interest if you do it in a positive way. You can accomplish all that by recruiting. I learned it, and it made me fortunes. So now I have three skills: milking cows, making sales, and recruiting.

**Another skill I learned was organizing, getting people to work together.** Once you have a few people to mentor, get them to work together. Getting people to work together is magic. Yes, it's it is also challenging. Having several members of your family, getting them to work together is challenging, but it's also exciting. Getting husband and wife to work together, it's challenging, but it's magic when it happens. Once you figure out the challenge and go for it, then the pieces fall into place.

Let me tell you how wonderful it is when people work together. Let me quote the Bible again. It says, "If two or three agree on a common purpose, nothing is impossible." Just try that on for your mental size. Everybody's looking for a challenge. Here's what I teach to adults and kids. The best challenge in the world: *Let's go do it.* Not you go do it. Let's go do it. If two or three of us decide on a common purpose, nothing's impossible. Working together, organizing.

When individuals are independent, it's a little more challenging. They each have their own opinions, their own ambitions and desires. It's challenging. But that's what makes life, the variety, the diversity of ideas and approaches and personalities.

Nevertheless, getting people to work together can be like herding cats. Sheep are easy to herd. But try herding cats.

But when you make it work and people are combining their attributes for a positive and united outcome, the power is so immense that you will be astounded at the success you all experience.

One of the powers of working together is shared testimonials. When people share their success testimonials, others are powerfully motivated.

***The skill I learned next was to reward people for progress.*** Rewarding people for small steps of progress gives them a sense of accomplishment. Sometimes, all it takes is a handshake, a pat on the back, a personal comment, "Mary, you're doing a fabulous job." Figure out how to get people to take the next and then the next step toward promotion. Urge them to do what they wouldn't ordinarily do by themselves. People will do some unique things if given enough encouragement. Maybe all that needs to be said is, "Mary, if you do this and this then..." She says, "Wow, I'll go for it." She might not have thought of that on her own.

Then there's ingenuity. Sales is representing a unique product, and getting customers, recruiting distributors, and promoting, and all this stuff. Ingenuity is figuring out a better way; if it doesn't work this way, we'll work another way. I used my ingenuity and made a fortune. My ingenuity worked for coming up with unique campaigns throughout each year.

For example, my ingenuity created a "schoolteacher week/month" campaign. I'd pick a category or career and say, "Let's go for it." And it doesn't matter what it is, just dream up something so that your recruits have an objective to go after rather than just their own pursuits. Key phrase, we all need to belong to something bigger than ourselves. As mentors, we furnish inspiration for what's bigger, and the bigger furnishes inspiration for us. I learned promotion, and it paid big money. You can too!

*Communication was the next learned skill.* Communication includes how to conduct a meeting. I learned identification, logic and reason, attack and confess, solution—simple aspects of communication. It wasn't easy for me at first. I stood up to give my first presentation and my mind sat back down. Have you ever been through that type of experience? I opened my mouth, and nothing came out for a while. But here's what I did—I did it again. I didn't give up. I stood up again and again and gave each presentation until I got comfortable doing it. That's the secret to how I got here 40 years later. I did it once, and it was uncomfortable. That first presentation was so lousy. But I did it again, and then I did it again, and then I did it again, and I did it again.

# Key phrase:
# Everyone needs to belong to something bigger than themselves.

I remember when I first decided to be a little more animated, and walk out away from the podium to be more personable, connect more with the audience. So I got out there, and then I thought, *How do you get back? Whoa, I'm stranded out here.* Do you remember those times, doing something for the first time? But you learn quickly in this business. A guy stands up to give his first testimonial, and he's so nervous he forgets his own name. Yet 30 days later, he wants to give a three-hour testimonial. You can hardly get him off the stage.

Learn good communication skills—how to affect people with words. That's the greatest art in the world to learn. Key phrase, don't be lazy with your language. When you learn to use the gift of language wisely, it can make you a fortune and build an incredible life.

**Another skill is to train people on how the business works.** Teaching is how life works. We all need for success in the 21st century are business skills and life skills. Life skills are leadership skills and learning how to set goals.

# Key phrase: Use the gift of language wisely.

*The ultimate skill to learn is the ability to inspire.* Inspiring people can transform your life and the life of whoever will listen. To inspire means to help people look up a little higher than where they are, and wish they could get there—inspire them to believe it's possible. We inspire by our own testimonial: "If I can do it, you can do it." We also inspire by sharing other people's testimonies. "If they can do it, Mary, you can do it." Getting people to see themselves better than they are. Getting people to see themselves richer than they are. Getting people to see themselves more capable next year than they are this year. Getting to see themselves in the future.

To help both your kids and your people, learn to help people see themselves as they are. If people have made mistakes, they have to know it. They can't continue to make mistakes and hope to achieve. Mistakes have to be corrected. You have to correct your people and your children. Help them see themselves as they are. If they mess up, say, "You've messed up, and so the next step is for you to…"

Some parents tell their kids they've messed up, and then they leave them in the mess. No. Parents need to say something like, "You've messed up, but here's what you could become with just a couple of changes in your (attitude…)." We must help our children see themselves as they are, but here's the greatest gift—to help our children see themselves better than they are. To transport them not only to see their mistakes, but transport them past their mistakes to the future, to see their opportunity, to see the person they can become.

My mentor gave me the great gift of helping me see myself better than I was. At first, it was difficult to see, but then I started to believe, and that's how I got here today. He said, "One of these days, Mr. Rohn, you'll walk into a room full of people and you will hear some of them say, 'That's him. That's the famous man I heard about.'"

"That could never happen to me."

He said, "Trust me. If you keep working hard on the disciplines like you're doing right now, that *will* happen. You'll walk into a room full of people and someone will say, 'That's him. That's the famous man I heard about.'"

He saw it, and he tried to get me to see it. And now, finally, it's happened. I think when I walked in here today, I heard someone say, "That's him—he's famous." It happened for me. And if it can happen for me, it can happen for you. Just master the skill to inspire.

# 12

# LEADERSHIP SKILLS FOR THE 21ST CENTURY

**W**e've reached the final chapter of our journey, and in many ways, we've come full circle in this book, *The Day That Turns Your Life Around*. A great deal of the content has focused on building the skills and the philosophical frameworks for making your dreams a reality.

But paradoxically, in the process of turning any area of your life around, a dramatic, almost mystical process occurs. You will become so skilled, so effective, so persuasive, so inspiring, and so confident that you will be called to serve others in ways that you can hardly imagine.

The day that turned your life around will contain within it the seeds that spawn the life change of many others within your reach. This very thing happened to me at age 25. I then worked hard on myself and now have the good fortune of helping others do the same.

Now you can learn those leadership lessons as well so you can carry the torch of life change to those you care about.

***Leadership Lesson: To attract attractive people, you must be attractive.*** In this context, being "attractive" doesn't mean physical appearance—it refers to attracting someone's attention because of an attribute or character trait. First of all, it is a good idea to ponder, *What would make me an attractive person?* I suggest that you would be attractive as a result of a refinement of philosophy so that you really understand life and challenge to the best of your ability. Your philosophy about the marketplace and politics and government and your work ethic. Your philosophy of values and contributions. Your philosophy that understands each of us need all of us, and all of us need each of us. Each value is important.

The miracle of the United States of America is all the gifts that have been flowing in for the past 400 years, especially the last 200 years. No country in the last 6,000 years has received as many gifts of citizens of the world as America has over the last 200 years. There's been nothing like it in recorded history. So many gifts from all around the whole world deposited in one country.

My grandparents came from Odesa, Russia, and settled in a place in the central part of the state of Washington in the United States where a lot of Germans settled. They called it Odessa, Washington, named after Odesa, Ukraine. My grandfather served in the tsar's army and they had a deal based on your deportment, you got certain points. If a soldier accumulated enough points, he got to put his name into a lottery. My grandfather accumulated enough points and participated in the lottery. Guess what happened to those who won these lotteries that they held every once in a while? The soldier could pick up his family and go to America. My grandfather won one of these lotteries! He and his one son and his wife moved to America. Odessa, Washington. And my father was born in Odessa, Washington. Interesting.

The gifts we have living in this country are multiplied millions over. People from all over the world have come here, and they didn't come empty-handed. They brought their recipes. They brought the work ethic. They brought the gift of language. They brought the gift of law. They brought the gift of music, the gift of medicine, the gift of healing. The United States of America is a wonderful composite of all the gifts of the world. The ethnic streams that have been flowing in here have made us great. Some parts of the world experience ethnic cleansing. Where would we even start here in this diverse country of ours? It's an amazing and rich mixture of cultures, religions, ethnicities, and much more. We need to participate in the gifts that America has.

The joy I have is to visit the lands where these gifts came from. I love to go to Italy, and I love to go to Poland, and I love to go to Czechoslovakia, and I love to go to Israel, and I love to go to all the places around the world—to see where America came from. And the gifts they brought here helped me to develop my gifts, and now I'm taking some of my gifts back to where they came from. Can you imagine the feeling of making a transcontinental contribution? Because they came here, now I go there. It's big-time for a farm kid from Idaho.

So to attract attractive people to work with you, you must be attractive. Work hard on yourself. Leadership is really the challenge to be better than mediocre, better than average. The step above. Not just to be above from an ego standpoint, but to step above so you can help others. Someone said, to lift someone up, you must be on higher ground. How true.

# Key phrase: Leadership is to be something better than mediocre.

The challenge of leadership to be something more than average or mediocre has these components:

- *Learn to be strong but not rude.* Strength, we need. Rudeness, we don't need. Here's where it's important to learn the graces, not just the skills.

- *Be kind but not weak.* Sometimes it's easy to mistake weakness for kindness but not true. Kindness is a powerful strength, but don't let your kindness become weakness.

- *Be bold but not a bully.* Boldness, we need. Bully, we don't need. Throwing weight around, we don't need. Trying to impress, we don't need. Express, yes. But impress, no.

- *Be thoughtful but not lazy.* To dream but not just become a dreamer. To think but not just become a thinker. To have a philosophy but not to become just a philosopher. I know they call me The Great Business Philosopher, which, I like the title. It's okay. But my philosophy says, jot it down, results is the name of the game. The name of the game is not philosophy. Philosophy is just a useful tool to set you on a good track so that a year from now you'll be in a better place than you would've on the old track. Maybe you will set a new track for your health, and for your family, and for your future, and for your activity, and for your productivity, and for your spirituality, and all the rest of good values. So, be thoughtful but not lazy.

- *Be proud but not arrogant*. Pride, we need. Team pride, and community pride, and state pride, and country pride, and personal pride, and family pride. But not arrogance. Don't let your pride slip into arrogance.

- *Be humble but not timid*. Some people mistake timidity for humility, but humility is a virtue. Timidity is an illness, a malady that can be corrected. You can learn to drive your timidity into such a small corner it does not now disturb the rest of the house. Be sophisticated. It doesn't take much to learn and practice the art of sophistication.

- *Have a sense of humor without folly*. Humor has its place, but just don't cross the line so that your humor becomes folly. It's okay to be witty but not silly. If you want to lead as a parent, and lead as a manager, and lead as an entrepreneur, if you want to lead as a community leader, and lead as a senator, and lead as an important person of influence and power, witty, yes. Silly, no.

Every leader must understand the law of averages so you can use it for your benefit and for your company, anything you might be involved in. The law of averages says if you do something often enough, you receive a ratio of results. And anyone can create this ratio. In baseball, we simply call it batting average. If you bat 10 times and get a hit, we say you're batting 100. And 3 hits out of 10, you're batting 300. You don't have to be perfect going up to bat. These days, batting 250 or 300, you can make $4 or $5 million a year.

In sales, that's about all you have to do. You don't need to bat 1,000. You don't need to bat perfect. You can get plenty of nos, but the yeses can make you rich. So don't worry about the nos. Concentrate on the yeses that make you rich. Key: once the ratio starts, it tends to continue. If you can get 1 yes out of 10 presentations, chances are if you give 10 more presentations, you will get another one. 10 more, you get another one. Next, the ratio can be improved. The fourth time you talk to 10 people, you get 2 instead of 1. Now you're starting to grow.

We must also understand the ratio and the law of averages when it comes to dealing with all the projects concerning human beings. Here's the simple ratio. Everything is a pyramid, and the reason is because all humans are different in temperament, desire, and goal-setting. If we attend university and count the number of freshmen, and count the number of sophomores, are there the same number of sophomores as freshmen? No. As many juniors as sophomores? No. As many seniors as juniors? No. Someone may say, "Well, shouldn't we fix this?" No. This is the way it is. Everybody's different, everybody has different ambitions. This is not a moral issue. Life takes its inevitable toll in college and in business.

Each human being has a different set of visions for their own future. Some people are willing to settle for more safety than risk. It's safer to be an employee than to be an entrepreneur. It's not a moral question between being an employee and an entrepreneur—it's usually a matter of temperament. And sometimes you have to be careful what you teach en masse because there's such a variety of personalities. Everybody should do the best they can with where they want to be. Sometimes, people linger for a long time in the freshman class, and then suddenly they decide to grow. Now they graduate, and become entrepreneurs, and bless the world. Who knows when those things will occur?

## KEEP LEARNING

I used to hope that everyone would have the same motivation. I hoped everyone would want to be extremely successful. I used to say, "I'm going to change these people if it kills me." I almost died. You can't change people unless they want to be changed. You'll learn early not to send ducks to eagle school. It's not a matter of morality or demeaning, it's just that everyone has their own definition of success and commitment. Our best encouragement is to do the best you can and keep learning about how your people think and what motivates them. Do the best you can.

One of the surprising discoveries I made is that people of modest means can become sophisticated. Learning sophistication and practicing it is not expensive. How much is a book on unique sophistication to bless your life? $30? It's not $3,000. It's not $30,000. How much is a library card? It's free. The study and practice of sophistication are available to everyone no matter their financial status. Know that wealth does not guarantee sophistication. Wealth doesn't guarantee the graces.

I know a rich guy. He's a clod. He eats with his elbow in his soup; he's a slob. His money has done nothing for him in terms of sophistication and uniqueness, and yet someone of very modest means can be very sophisticated. They know the graces. They live a unique life even though they have modest means. It's interesting. Let everybody do whatever they wish to do, but encourage everybody to do better. But let people linger if they wish to linger. Let them grow if they wish to grow. Help them change if they wish to change.

Another leadership skill to put into practice is to *work with the people who deserve it, not the people who need it.* We must operate like life operates. Life was designed not to give us what we need. Life was designed to give us what we deserve. And if you have people to work with, work with the ones who deserve it.

The next skill that's very important for a leader and management to understand is to *teach people how to deserve your time.* Teach people how to deserve your help. For example, say, "John, if you'll do this and this, I'll do all of this. And if you'll do that, and that, and that, I will do all of this. I will meet you more than halfway, but you have to come toward the halfway part. And probably, since I'm so anxious to work with you, if you'll start taking these steps, I'll probably meet you more than halfway." Leaders learn not to go all the way just because of need unless someone needs to be rescued. Unless the situation is out of control and there's no other way. Yes.

Next, leaders don't expect a pear tree to bear apples. I used to try to change everything. You can hang apples on a pear tree. But I'm telling you, it won't help. You can put up a sign, "This is an apple tree." Sure enough, come the season, pears appear. Here's what I learned. You cannot change people, but they can change themselves.

Capital in your business isn't what matters. It's not the money that buys you a future. It's your skills that buy you a future. Money and no skills, and I'm telling you, you're still poor. Money and no ambition, where are you? Money and no courage, you're broke. A little bit of money and a whole lot of courage. That's all you need.

Back in my recruiting days, I was looking for people, the money didn't matter. What mattered to me was somebody's willingness, somebody's ingenuity, somebody's willingness to try. If they had a dollar to invest, that was plenty for me. A dollar and some ambition, and I can show you how to get rich, and it'll be one of the classic stories of the company.

When I went to recruit somebody and they said, "I don't have any money," I said, "I've been looking for you for six months. Let me show you how to do it without any money because here are the rules of capitalism—you can either buy and sell, or if you're in certain circumstances, you can sell and buy. If you have ambition. Now if you don't have any ambition, we can't cure that. And money won't cure lack of ambition. But if you have a dollar and some ambition, I'll show you how to get rich. And even if you don't have a dollar, I'll show you how to get rich because you can sell and buy.

Every leader must understand the story of the frog and the scorpion, which represents good and evil. Adults and kids alike must study the story of the frog and the scorpion. The story says the scorpion and the frog appeared on the bank of the river at about the same time, and the frog was about to jump into the river and swim to the other side. But before the frog jumped, the scorpion came up and said, "Mr. Frog, I wish to get to the other side of the river. I'm a scorpion, and I can't swim. Would you be so kind to let me hop on your back, and you swim across the river and deposit me on the other side?"

The frog looked at the scorpion and said, "No way. Scorpions sting frogs and kill them. I'd get out there halfway, and you'd sting me, and I'd drown."

And the scorpion says, "Hey, with your frog brain, you're not thinking. If I stung you out there halfway across the river, yes, you would die, but so would I. I'm not interested in committing suicide. I want to get to the other side, please."

The frog says, "Okay, that makes sense. Hop on."

So the scorpion hops on the frog's back, starts across the river. Sure enough, halfway across the river, the scorpion stings the frog. They are now both in the water about to go down for the third time. The frog could not believe what had happened and said to the scorpion, "Why did you do that? I'm about to drown, but so are you. Why did you do that?"

And the scorpion says, "Because I am a scorpion."

You have to understand the story of the frog and the scorpion, which leads you to understand human nature.

Here's what the prophet said, "Beware of the little foxes that eat the vines." You look at the vines, and everything looks okay. You look a little closer and see that the little foxes have been busy, and you soon will not have a vineyard. You cannot entertain evil in any respect.

You say, "Well, a little of this or that won't hurt." A little begins the process. Even with some productive people, you would do better without them because they may be the scorpion. You must do the work of father, the protector, and the work of mother to nourish. The battle is always raging, and you must be wise. Be careful what you sow because the evil side of life reaps the whirlwind.

I wrote this book to invest a piece of my life into your life, and I expect a miracle to occur. And I expect it to multiply, and multiply, and multiply. No telling how far these ideas, the notes you've taken, may spread and go and go. One generation to the next, to the next. It is so fantastic to comprehend. But sometimes when you sow, you don't reap. You must be prepared for that. Once in a while, things are upside-down. Once in a while, the economy goes into a tailspin. Once in a while, it doesn't work. But let me give you the promise that when opportunity knocks, take the chance. We always have another chance, as human beings, to participate in the miracle process to help change somebody's life. Rescue somebody from oblivion. Build an organization second-to-none, so that your name will appear in many people's testimony.

Because you've taken notes and completed the workshop and have read all the chapters in this book, you have all you need to turn your life around. I encourage you to take the next steps to live the life you dream about.

Start today!

# CONCLUSION

What do you really want out of life? It's a big question. In many ways, it's a very personal question. But when you get right down to it, as different as we all are, the things we're searching for in life are essentially the same. You want to be happy. You want to feel good. You want to enjoy the time you've been given. You want a job you really love. You want the relationships in your life to be healthy, and enriching, and wonderful. You want enough money so that you don't have to worry about money. You want to develop the skills to do something meaningful with your life. Something that contributes to the world in a positive way and fulfills your sense of purpose. By reading this book you've discovered that information does exist to help you become skilled in one area of your life.

Now, you can get the information to become skilled in absolutely anything. Even your spirituality can be strengthened by developing the right skills. And skills, quite simply, are the secret to success. Ask anyone who has ever achieved their dreams. They'll tell you that skills are the key. Many people never learn these kinds of life skills because they're not taught in school. You have to go out and get them on your own. But where do you go? The fact that you're reading this book now means you're already part of the way there. Why not go all the way?

# ABOUT JIM ROHN
## (1930-2009)

For more than 40 years, Jim Rohn honed his craft like a skilled artist—helping people the world over sculpt life strategies that expanded their imagination of what is possible. Those who had the privilege of hearing him speak can attest to the elegance and common sense of his material.

So, it is no coincidence that he is still widely regarded as one of the most influential thinkers of our time, and thought of by many as a national treasure. He authored numerous books and audio and video programs and helped motivate and shape an entire generation of personal development trainers and hundreds of executives from America's top corporations.

# THANK YOU FOR READING THIS BOOK!

If you found any of the information helpful, please take a few minutes and leave a review on the bookselling platform of your choice.

## BONUS GIFT!

Don't forget to sign up to try our newsletter and grab your free personal development ebook here:

soundwisdom.com/classics

# GET ALL 3 BOOKS
## AND TAKE CONTROL
## OF YOUR LIFE!

Available everywhere books are sold.

# ALSO BY JIM ROHN...

Embark on a transformative journey with Jim Rohn's *The Art of Exceptional Living*. This succinct guide, segmented into focused chapters, offers invaluable insights on personal development, goal setting, and forging a unique path in life. Rohn, with his personal and often humorous anecdotes, encourages readers to evaluate their lifestyles, urging them to become the best versions of themselves. A book that promises not just wealth but an enrichment of life's value, steering you towards a fulfilling path of self-betterment and happiness. Start living exceptionally today with Rohn's profound wisdom.

**AVAILABLE EVERYWHERE BOOKS ARE SOLD**

Discover the transformative power of true ambition with Jim Rohn's groundbreaking book, *The Power of Ambition*. Rohn, a revered authority on success, guides you on a path to harnessing your innermost drive to foster personal achievement and uplift those around you. Through six pioneering strategies, you'll learn to cultivate a disciplined and eager desire that propels you toward your goals while serving others. From mastering resilience to effective networking, this comprehensive guide is a masterclass in building a life filled with passion and purpose.

**AVAILABLE EVERYWHERE BOOKS ARE SOLD**

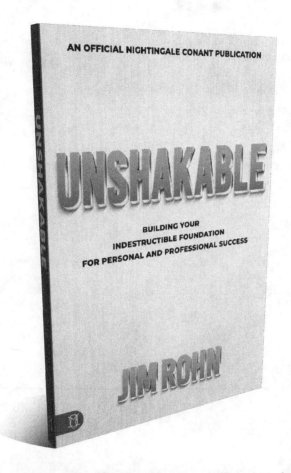

AN OFFICIAL NIGHTINGALE CONANT PUBLICATION

# UNSHAKABLE

BUILDING YOUR
INDESTRUCTIBLE FOUNDATION
FOR PERSONAL AND PROFESSIONAL SUCCESS

## JIM ROHN

Unlock your potential and pave the road to personal and professional success with *Unshakable*, the famous tour de force from the distinguished Jim Rohn. Drawing from over four decades of insights into human behavior, Rohn presents twelve fundamental qualities to forge an unshakable character that magnetizes success. With captivating insights and actionable strategies, it's your indispensable companion in crafting a rewarding future grounded in steadfast principles. Take the first step towards becoming *Unshakable* — a version of yourself that is grounded, resilient, and primed for success in all life's avenues.

**AVAILABLE EVERYWHERE BOOKS ARE SOLD**